ONE LORD, ONE FAITH

ONE LORD, ONE' FAITH

Getting back to the basics of
your Christianity in
an age of confusion

PETER C. MOORE

THOMAS NELSON PUBLISHERS
Nashville

Published in Nashville, Tennessee, by Thomas Nelson, Inc., Publishers, and distributed in Canada by Word Communications, Ltd., Richmond, British Columbia.

The Bible version used in this publication is THE NEW KING JAMES VERSION. Copyright © 1979, 1980, 1982, Thomas Nelson, Inc., Publishers. Scripture quotations noted NASB are from the New American Standard Bible, © 1960, 1962, 1963, 1968, 1971, 1972, 1973, 1975, 1977 by The Lockman Foundation. Used by permission.

Library of Congress Cataloging-in-Publication Data

Moore, Peter C., 1936–
    One Lord, one faith / Peter C. Moore.
        p. cm.
    Includes bibliographical references.
    ISBN 0-8407-9211-5 (pbk.)
    1. Apologetics. 2. Apostles' Creed.
BT1102.M654 1994
239—dc20   93–35859
                                                     CIP

Printed in the United States of America.
1 2 3 4 5 6 — 99 98 97 96 95 94

For the people of

Little Trinity Church, Toronto,

from whom I have learned

far more than I have taught

Father in Heaven! What is a human being without thee! What is all that one knows, vast accumulation though it be, but a chipped fragment if one does not know thee! What is all striving, could it ever encompass a world, but a half-finished work if one does not know thee: thee the One, who art one thing and who art all! So may thou give to the intellect, wisdom to comprehend that one thing; to the heart, sincerity to receive this understanding; to the will, purity that wills only one thing. In prosperity may thou grant perseverance to will one thing; amid distractions, collectedness to will one thing; in suffering, patience to will one thing. Oh, thou that givest both the beginning and the completion, may thou early, at the dawn of day, give to the young person the resolution to will one thing. As the day wanes, may thou give the older person a renewed remembrance of the first resolution, that the first may be like the last, the last like the first, in possession of a life that has willed only one thing.

Sören Kierkegaard

The Prayers of Kierkegaard

CONTENTS

ACKNOWLEDGMENTS

Many people have helped in the production of this book whom I wish to thank. First, the people of Little Trinity Church for their attentiveness to the content of the Christian faith and their concern for live orthodoxy. Then I want to mention especially Denyse O'Leary, my local editor, whose suggestions as to content, wording, and approach have been invaluable to me. Marcia Sands, William Samarin, and John Webster all read the manuscript and gave me thoughtful comments, and Brian Hampton, my Thomas Nelson editor, has sharpened my thought and phraseology in many places. I am deeply indebted also to my family for the time they have given me to complete this manuscript. Finally, I am grateful to the many people whose stories are included in the text. Thanks to them, they have made the faith come alive to me in ways that are both fresh and diverse.

THE
APOSTLES'
CREED

I believe in God, the Father almighty, maker of heaven and earth;

And in Jesus Christ his only Son our Lord; who was conceived by the Holy Ghost, born of the Virgin Mary, suffered under Pontius Pilate, was crucified, dead, and buried; he descended into hell; the third day he rose again from the dead; he ascended into heaven, and sitteth on the right hand of God the Father almighty; from thence he shall come to judge the quick and the dead.

I believe in the Holy Ghost, the holy catholic Church, the communion of saints, the forgiveness of sins, the resurrection of the body, and the life everlasting. Amen.

1

Encountering Truth
in a
Relativistic Age

Perhaps because I worked for twenty-five years in America's private secondary schools (now in our more egalitarian times called *independent schools*), I enjoy trying to guess which campus Hollywood chooses as backdrops for its films about teenagers trapped behind the ivy walls of privilege and emotional deprivation. I was delighted, then, when I recognized the neo-gothic backdrop for *Dead Poets Society* as the campus of St. Andrew's School in Middletown, Delaware.

I had visited the school often when I worked as director of a small, national, religious organization. My job was to strengthen the spiritual life of its three hundred member schools across the nation; thus I had spoken in the chapel and met with student groups and knew the headmaster well because he was the chair of my board of trustees.

Watching the film brought back memories of a conference I helped organize at St. Andrew's in 1972. The setting was tranquil and idyllic: The boys were away on spring vacation, and banks of daffodils, dormant during the winter months, were pushing through the gently rolling grounds. Some one hundred twenty headmasters, headmistresses, and faculty had assembled for a conference on the subject of religion and values.

Among the speakers invited was Senator Harold Hughes, three-term governor of Iowa, outspoken critic of the Vietnam war, and a Democratic leader in Congress. Hughes was also a committed Christian. The Senator gave a remarkable speech at the conference, one which provided a striking contrast between the Christian's answer to life's tragedies and senselessness and the romantic solution so dramatically articulated in the film by the teacher, played by Robin Williams.

A Miracle at the Racquet Club

Senator Hughes's address was a simple but powerful testimony of his response to his daughter's death, his own alcoholism (from which he was still recovering), and of the grace and power of Christ to redeem broken lives. The room was very quiet. One sensed that many of these educators either had never heard such an honest and dynamic witness or, if they had, that it didn't fit well into the familiar, pressured world of college admissions, fund-raising, and interscholastic sports. I recall an almost palpable sense of peace filling the room as these educators, gathered from a wide variety of religious and secular traditions, listened to the Senator conclude his talk by recounting a recent experience in New York City.

The Senator had met at the exclusive Racquet Club on Manhattan's East Side with a group of Middle Eastern ambassadors to the United Nations, including Arabs, an Israeli, and several Westerners. Together, the group struggled with issues of justice and peace. Because the Palestinian issue was foremost in their minds, the air bristled with tension. While all were eager for peace, they were poles apart in seeing how to achieve it. But they talked for a good while in as friendly a way as one could expect under the circumstances. While the atmosphere was cordial, even at times warm, the group remained unreconciled, and a sense of futility began to take over.

Perceiving the impasse, the Senator used his role as the chair to take a bold tack. He spent a few minutes sharing with the group his own spiritual pilgrimage, of how God's gracious help had enabled him to come to terms with two things utterly beyond his control, namely his daughter's recent death and his own struggle with alcoholism. All were listening intently. Then, as the meeting came to a close, Senator Hughes suggested that they do something unconventional: stand in a circle, hold hands, and pray. All obliged.

Quietly and very naturally, he prayed an extemporaneous prayer, thanking God for each person in the room, and asking for that peace and understanding which only God could give. It was brief and to the point; and as simply as he had begun, he concluded by naming Jesus as the one in whom all people find unity and love. When he opened his eyes, he saw that there was hardly a dry eye in the room.

My heart was in my throat as the Senator related this incident to our conference. Under normal circumstances, so personal a witness would have made this crowd uneasy. But in a very natural way Hughes continued to explain that just as Christ had given him power over alcohol, Christ had brought unity to that divided group, enabling the seemingly impossible to happen. Impenetrable barriers came down, and those ambassadors—Muslims, Jews, and Westerners—who only moments before had been far apart, were suddenly drawn together in God's loving embrace. The story, second hand as it was, had a power that left the conference stunned.

A Different Drummer?

The conference and the film happened at the same location, but they represent two opposing answers to the question of how one finds truth in a world of competing ideologies. In *Dead Poets Society* Robin Williams plays an attractive, dynamic teacher dropped down into the world of a boys' school in the 1950s, where unimaginative education and oppressive morals masquerade as virtue. To him these children of privilege are locked into a straitjacket of mindless social and intellectual conformity. He longs to help them break out and find themselves. He attempts to help them do this by an appeal to the Romantic poets, using his unique pedagogical skill to stir a deep responsive chord in the minds of his impressionable students. In one memorable scene he takes his class to a flagstone courtyard and says: "Now, I want you to march." Instantly forming themselves into a neat row, the respectful boys set out in perfect lockstep. "No," Williams says, "don't march together, march any way you want." At first the boys don't understand, but then with the abandon of escapees from prison, they march, dance, and parade, each to his own tune.

For the teacher in the film, and I assume for the makers of the film, truth is a product of freedom. For Senator Hughes, freedom is a product of truth. The teacher's vision, grounded in the romantic ideal of nonconformity, invites us to celebrate our diversity as in itself the path toward enlightenment. The Senator's vision, grounded in a deeply Christian impulse toward unity and reconciliation, offers truth from God as the light by which we find the freedom to love those who are different from us. This difference has a bearing on the problems we face when we examine the Christian faith as it relates to the secular world today.

Enthronement of Choice

Our modern culture has certainly opted for the view that equates freedom with unrestricted personal choice rather than for the vision of a truth that sets us free to love. Freedom has become simply a synonym for choice.

The enemy is likely to be pluralism, relativism, humanism, or the mysteries of the New Age.

Consequently, unity seems not only harder to achieve but more difficult to define. Communal ways of thinking or acting are regarded with suspicion, especially if there is even a hint of imposition from above. The problem is, as Robert Bellah and his team of sociologists observed in *Habits of the Heart,* how people forge bonds of attachment or cooperation when the entire social world is thought to be made up of individuals, each endowed with the right to be free of others' demands. Bonds imply obligations, and obligations impinge on one's freedom![1]

Even the great centers of learning, once purporting to be scholarly communities united in pursuit of truth, have caved in to the new pluralism. In his freshman address to the incoming class of 1993, Benno Schmidt, then president of Yale, described the dominant principle of a university as being freedom of thought. He decried the 1742 vision of Jonathan Edwards, one of Yale's illustrious graduates, of a university as a place where students would be trained to love both God and the good. Schmidt, who sees absolutes as "suffocating straitjackets," even questioned whether there is any ultimate truth for the university to pursue. The only moral right he accepted as axiomatic was the moral right to question whether there are moral rights. One can only ask why engage in education at all if the goal, namely truth, is so questionable. At one time skepticism was directed at uncovering error in the pursuit of truth. Now skepticism has replaced truth as the object of our quest. No wonder the modern institution is more a "pluriversity" than a university.[2]

The Great Divide

Given the smorgasbord of ideas our culture blesses by invoking the ultimate transcendence of choice, the temptation is simply to withdraw into a private, Christian world and cradle one's faith in the safe confines of church and home. Too many believers combine this withdrawal with an appalling ignorance about the Christian faith itself. Decades ago British novelist Dorothy Sayers said that the average Christian is about as equipped to do battle with a convinced Marxist as a boy with a peashooter facing a nest of machine guns. Today, the enemy is less likely to be Marxism (save on the campuses of some Western universities) than it is to be pluralism, relativism, humanism, or the mysteries of the New Age—but the average Christian is just as ill-prepared.[3]

Compounding this problem are the many voices claiming to guide the modern Christian into an enlightened approach to doctrine freed from excessive loyalty to the past. These "prophets" claim to have discovered new truths which must be set alongside the classical sources of Scripture, tradition, and sanctified reason—or even replace them. The challenge to believers can be very troubling, but it must be faced honestly and surmounted.

Against the backdrop of such a divided culture, the Christian expectation of unity in belief and confession appears to some to be an unwelcome anachronism. "Doctrine divides," goes the old slogan; and anyone with even a cursory knowledge of church history knows that it often does. Wouldn't life be simpler if each of us could have a private faith that answered life's basic questions for us personally, but did not oblige us to try to get others to conform to our views? Such an approach would be simpler, but it would not be Christianity. Christian faith is intensely personal, but it is *not* private. While I must make faith my own, it neither begins nor remains my own because I share it with all those down through the centuries and across the continents who have found in Christ the way, the truth, and the life. But the reaction to such united witness in some quarters is fierce. Many think that the only way to preserve some semblance of community within our modern context of diversity is to replace the quest for truth with the pursuit of tolerance.

Does tolerance build community? It is often pointed out that, without some generally accepted myth, people simply do not coalesce. Everywhere we see the old nation-states breaking up along ethnic lines. When the center no longer holds, as Yeats predicted in 1916 in his famous poem, "The Second Coming," "Things fall apart . . . Mere anarchy is loosed upon the world."

The church is thus faced with two threats: One from without, calling into question the validity of its claim to have found truth; the other from within, pressuring it to embrace a more accommodating approach to the pluralism found in secular culture. Both threats cause fragmentation, but thereby they force us to rethink the doctrine we Christians share. Only a common vision prevents groups from breaking apart into countless, incompatible fragments.[4]

Conformity vs. Community

The Christian community we seek is not simply a Christian "clan." Indeed, the temptation to become cliquish is a powerful one in many circles. One response to the disintegration of modern life is not to withdraw into an entirely private world but to seek refuge within groups where people share a common viewpoint. Christians are often strong advocates of this trend. One Baptist church in Texas boasts 64 softball teams, 48 basketball teams, 84 volleyball teams, golf tournaments, fitness clubs, craft groups, and a 500-member choir. All this is housed in a multi-purpose facility which includes racquetball courts, weight and aerobic rooms, six bowling lanes, and a year-round snack bar. It would seem that you can live almost your whole life there without ever having to meet anyone who isn't a Baptist![5]

In these affinity groups there is doubtless a surface conviviality, but underneath there is often stifling conformity. The insecurity prevents members from building natural bridges to other communities. By contrast, the church, when it really is the church, is linked by bonds more historical and more personal than those achieved by participation in shared social activities. The church is linked by a common faith in Jesus Christ. In fact, this defines what the church really is. The church consists of those within each generation who proclaim that truth is a given, that it was "once for all delivered" through the prophets, apostles, and historians who wrote the Bible. The church is that people who together understand the world through the prism of biblical faith.

Does this sound intolerably exclusive? Historically, biblical Christianity has always been regarded as such. Even before the Bible took its final written form, the earliest Christian proclamation, "Jesus is Lord," sounded a surprisingly exclusive note in a pluralistic world. Jewish society, where the proclamation was first heard, was itself highly fragmented. There were many groups and parties: political revolutionaries (the Zealots); religious purists (the Essenes); legalistic reactionaries (the Pharisees); moderating realists (the Sadducees);

monarchists (the "party of Herod"); and accultu-
rated synthesizers (the Hellenists). Each group re-
acted differently to Christian preaching, although
all agreed that the new believers were a troublesome messianic sect. As Christians moved beyond
Judaism into the Gentile world they encountered an
even more bewildering array of world views: mystery cults, early gnostic groups, remnants of the old
Greek and Roman worship, animism and supersti-
tion, and, of course, the cult of the divine emperor.
There were even personal and household gods to
fulfill the need for more intimate contact with the
higher powers.

This is not to minimize some important differences between the world of the first century and
the world today. For example, despite great religious
diversity, the relativistic notion that each person
should be entitled to his or her own truth, so pervasive today, would not have occurred to most of these
strangers to the gospel. Personal pieties were one
thing; private meddling with state religion was not
allowed. However, Rome had worked out a policy of
"live and let live" so that major religious groups
could practice according to their consciences without threat of official repression. Judaism was permitted to flourish as long as it did not threaten
political stability.

As long as Christianity was viewed as a sect
within Judaism it, too, was granted protection.
Once the clear proclamation of the uniqueness of
Jesus and His supremacy over the Jewish Law became a problem for Jewish communities through-

out the Roman world, however, Christians had to fend for themselves. Christianity looked so Jewish and yet wasn't; it became a target for Jewish anger and was easily implicated in riots and disorders. Fundamentally, however, Christians were persecuted because their teachings were exclusive; boldly they proclaimed that there was only one way to forgiveness and eternal life: Jesus Christ.

The Limits of Tolerance

In effect, the early Christians were arguing for a certain kind of intolerance. They were prepared to be tolerant of the political and legal system of the majority culture. In this respect they were tolerant even to a fault, some say, in that they failed to attack the institution of slavery.[6] Christians were also willing to be socially tolerant, mingling freely with neighbors whom they hoped to win for Christ. Christian homes were centers of worship and evangelism, where inquiring pagans were often welcomed.[7] But when it came to intellectual tolerance of viewpoints which had been identified in the apostles' writings as error—that was another matter.

Within the New Testament churches there was a protracted struggle over precisely what apostolic faith included and excluded. Various forms of accommodation with the non-Christian religions of the day were first suggested and then outlawed. It was to distinguish authentic faith from counterfeit doctrines that the Apostles' and the Nicene Creeds were composed and subsequently incorporated into the regular worship life of the Christian community. These creeds, as well as others, served many purposes. They reinforced orthodoxy, served as outlines of basic biblical beliefs to be learned by catechumens (those seeking to become new members), and provided liturgical acts by which the community's common faith was celebrated as a gift from God.

Today intolerance in any form is widely rejected on a theoretical basis because it offends the reigning philosophy of pluralism. Yet in practice, various forms of "politically correct" thinking are imposed upon communities of learning through group pressure, sometimes culminating in the denial of basic rights like freedom of speech. Ironically, such persecution by the politically correct is generally done in the name of tolerance! All of which leads one to conclude that tolerance serves well as one quality of a healthy cultural climate, but poorly as an overarching goal for the culture.

It is helpful to remember that the idea of tolerance includes the willingness to accept another's belief in an idea of which one does not approve. Christians are tolerant of other faiths in the sense that they are willing to allow others to believe them. But the historian Arnold Toynbee was wrong when he thought that the only way to purge Christianity of sinful exclusivism and intolerance was to shed the traditional belief that Christianity is unique.[8] Toynbee was confusing tolerance with pluralism. The one does not necessarily imply the other. In fact, logically there is no need for tolerance toward

a viewpoint with which one agrees. One only toler-
ates a viewpoint with which one disagrees.[9] The
call for tolerance is often simply a smoke screen
for synthesizing Christianity defined by the Creeds
with non-Christian ideas.

Designer Religion

Another factor which works against efforts to
build a Christian community of belief is the current
trend toward *designer religion*. Holding to one base
of truth amidst a great variety of options goes
against the trend of tailor-made religion. Recent
studies have shown that the religious revival predicted by such futurists as Alvin Toffler and John
Naisbitt has already begun. Baby boomers are re-
turning to churches and synagogues.[10] There is a
widespread hunger for meaning, but many bring
an aversion to such traditional concepts as sin, forgiveness, commitment, even truth itself. One has
articulated the idea as, "Instead of me fitting a religion, I found a religion to fit me."[11]

Tempting though it may be to have large congregations again, the church must not rearrange its
message to suit those who want a faith to satisfy
their *"felt needs."* To do so only puts the church at
the service of some other spirit than the Holy Spirit.
Joy Davidman found this to be true. Known both
for her writings and a pilgrimage from atheism to
faith that led her to marry C. S. Lewis, Davidman
wrote: "We must return to Christianity in order to
preserve the things we value. But we cannot return

to Christianity at all unless the thing we value above all else is Christ. . . . Otherwise, we are in effect, asking Christ to save our idols for us."[12]

> **The call for tolerance is often simply a smoke screen for synthesizing Christianity.**

Those who change the gospel to fit the cultural expectations of the age must face challenges like the one recently put forward by two Duke University theologians, Stanley Hauerwas and William Willimon. They point out that all such "apologists" are heirs to a theological tradition that mistakenly saw its task as making Jesus relevant to the age. But Jesus insisted that the age be relevant to Him. The task of the faithful Christian teacher is not to make the gospel "credible" to the world, but to make the world believe the gospel.[13]

Five Musts of the Modern Revisionist

We cannot simply dismiss the views of those who insist that basic Christian doctrines be revised to fit the age. To do so would be to fail to see that truth must always be defended against error. This is never more so than when the enemy is not blatant falsehood but a tolerant receptivity to any view except that which is orthodox. Let us take a moment to examine the assumptions of the revisionist.

The first assumption of the revisionist is that Scripture must be relativized. This means that the Word of God must be separated from the words of Scripture. Rejecting the classical hermeneutical principle that revelation is progressive and cumulative, which is, that God revealed only as much of Himself as was appropriate to Hebrew culture at a given time and that further revelation was a consistent unfolding of earlier themes, the revisers separate the New Testament from the Old, Jesus from

> **Instead of permitting the Bible to critique social trends, the revisionist critiques the Bible.**

the Gospels, the Gospels from Paul, the early Paul from the later Paul, and so on. The gospel is reduced to Jesus' loving commitment to others, to which Scripture is seen as an inadequate and often faulty witness. In the end, as Anglican theologian J. V. Langmead Casserley once said, the Bible becomes the Word of God from which comes no word of God.

Second, in the revisionist's view great weight must be placed on current insights from the social sciences. Opinions about homosexuality, the prevalence of out-of-wedlock liaisons of all kinds, the healthiness of divorce, the rejection of hierarchies, and the struggles of the oppressed are placed alongside the Bible as if they had equal authority to define ethical imperatives and shape church policies. These trends define a new culture, radically discontinuous with the assumptions of the Bible. Instead of permitting the Bible to critique them, the revisionist critiques the Bible.

Third, a new language for God must be found which transcends images, metaphors, and analogies. The revelations of Scripture are believed to be so culture-bound that they tie the faith irredeemably to the past. Since God is assumed to be beyond all such language, new gender-neutral or gender-inclusive language must be employed in liturgies and the Bible. Thus God is defined according to personal religious experience rather than an "outmoded" definition of God imposed on religious experience. This, of course, ties the Bible to a particular culture in our own day and the revisers thereby fall into the very trap they wish to avoid.

Fourth, the Spirit must be set free from any exclusive attachment to Jesus in order to become the guiding light of contemporary movements deemed to be politically correct. Instead of witnessing to Jesus Christ as the only Son of God, the Spirit is believed to baptize movements which will bring equality, peace, economic and political liberation, and pan-religious syncretism.[14]

Finally, all who oppose these proposals for "modernizing" Christianity must be caricatured as obstructive or obscurantist. Traditional believers are caricatured as literalistic, rigid, divisive, fundamentalist, and authoritarian—an awesome litany of evils from which even the most courageous would flee! It is they who are standing in the way of bringing the church into relevant dialogue with the modern world, and they who are insulating the Word of God from the work of "responsible" scholars and interpreters.[15]

I well recall a painful encounter during a private tutorial with my modernist professor at Oxford University. He discovered that I had chosen to argue for a traditional approach to an issue of biblical criticism rather than his favored contemporary one. Instead of calmly seeking to bring me to a more enlightened view, he flushed red in the face, jumped to the edge of his chair, asked me to stop reading my essay, and declared, "I am going to fight you on this all the way." It was an eye-opening experience for a young theological student just over from America!

Truth and Life

The chapters that follow are an attempt to define the basic core of Christian belief. This is not an exposition of the Apostles' Creed, although phrases from the Apostles' Creed form a framework for each chapter. Others far more qualified have expounded the Creed admirably and exhaustively.[16] Rather, this volume is a defense and interpretation of traditional Christian belief in the light of some of the contemporary challenges facing it. Heavier theological sections are interspersed with stories and illustrations from people's experiences, for biblical faith is also living truth.

Orthodoxy is not only true but also alive and

relevant to every age. Those with an aversion to thinking deeply about their faith may find the following chapters ponderous. Others who disagree may, at points, find them offensive. But the future is clear: unless all of us are prepared to think deeply about what we believe the day will be lost to those who glibly use Christian language and symbols to perpetrate a religion very different from the historic Christian faith.[17]

Truth is never merely intellectual. "The heart makes the theologian," said John Calvin. From ancient times, Hebrews thought that truth was not only to be learned, but also to be lived. Biblical truth is rarely found in isolation from the believing community. We encounter truth only when we are willing to be part of a people who are seeking to live under the lordship of Christ. The essence of these chapters was originally given orally to my congregation in Toronto, and their critical responses have been immeasurably important to the development of this book. The questions at the end of each chapter are aimed at stimulating the same kind of ongoing interaction that encourages application of truth.

Tradition vs. Traditionalism

I suspect that many readers grew up as I did, repeating the Apostles' Creed in worship services but only half understanding its meaning or historical significance. To the unawakened mind it seems only a piece of outmoded traditionalism. But as one of the church's earliest creedal statements, it has served as a reminder that truth is discovered, not only in the present but also in dialogue with the past. Yale theologian Jaraslov Pelikan has drawn a crucial distinction: "Whereas traditionalism is the dead religion of the living; tradition is the living religion of the dead."

Creeds have a place in Christian worship because they not only express the common beliefs of the faithful; they also offer those beliefs to God as an act of praise. Orthodoxy means literally "the right kind of glory." The Creed does far more than define doctrine accurately; it helps to glorify the God who has revealed Himself to us in Jesus Christ. A creed recited ensemble is a kind of prayer that properly ends with *Amen*. As Charles de Foucauld said: "Prayer is thinking about God while loving him." When we say the Creed aright, we express our love to God.

Moreover, as the New Testament writers were at pains to point out, belief and practice belong together (see James 1:22–26; Rom. 12). Nothing has titillated the skeptical world in recent years so much as the disgrace of highly visible believers whose libidos and greed outstripped their faith. By the same token, nothing so challenges the secular world as seeing Christianity faithfully put into practice. Since faith and life are two sides of a coin, what reason is there to believe that Christian living will persist after Christian faith is eroded?

Latin American theologians have pointed to the distinction between *orthodoxy* and *orthopraxis*. The one is what one claims to believe; the other is what one demonstrates as believing. To Jesus, the two were so intimately interconnected that only an orthodoxy allied to orthopraxis would pass the supreme test at the end of the age (see Matt. 7:21–27; 25:31–46). Any successful study of truth must begin with a humble openness before God and an earnest willingness to live for Him. The beginning must be like the prayer of Augustine in the fourth century:

O God, the light of every heart that sees Thee, the Life of every soul that loves Thee, the strength of every mind that seeks Thee, the house of my soul is too narrow for Thee, enlarge it; it is ruinous, repair it; it has that within which must offend Thee, cleanse it. Be Thou alone the joy of my heart. Amen.[18]

—Augustine

Questions for Discussion

1. What are the strengths and weaknesses of romantic individualism as an approach to life?

2. Has doctrine been a divisive or a unifying factor in your family and church?

3. Should churches be multiethnic or mono-ethnic? What are the advantages and disadvantages of each situation?

4. What are some of the idols today which people want Christ to save for them?

5. Should the gospel be relevant to the modern age, or vice versa?

An Eternal
Contradiction?

God, the Father almighty

Is it still appropriate to call God "Father" or are they correct who say that to call God "Father, Son, and Holy Spirit" is hopelessly outdated? Surprising though it may seem, many argue that, in place of traditional trinitarian terms, we must now use gender-inclusive words like "Creator, Redeemer, Sanctifier," or "Shepherd, Helper, Refuge," or even neutral terms like "The Ultimate, the Intimate, and Warmth." Radical feminist theologians insist we go a step further: "The Mother, the Child, and the Spirit."

In one new translation of the Bible, published by the National Council of Churches in the USA, John 1:14 describes Jesus not as "the only begotten Son of the Father" but as "the only Child of the Father and Mother."[1] Pressure to move in this direction is found within most mainline churches. At an Anglican conference I attended a woman priest led us in an "updated" version of the Lord's Prayer which began: "Our God, Father and Mother of us all, holy be Your name."

The Demise of Patriarchy

Behind these innovations lies a deep-seated conviction that the biblical message is encased in the thought forms of ancient patriarchal society. In order to speak afresh to the current age, it must be reshaped to fit in with the new understanding of the equality of the sexes. To see God as *Father* is not only an anachronism, it is positively harmful, considering the many people who have had painful, wounding experiences of human fatherhood.

At one point I decided to test this assumption with a young friend named Justin. When I first met Justin ten years ago, he was the epitome of an alienated teenager: heavily involved with drugs, skeptical about the God he had been taught to believe in as a child, and wild and disheveled in his appearance.

Over the course of years, Justin had come a long way. Now he was neat, well-dressed, enthusiastically active in Christian ministry to young people, and showing every sign of being at peace with himself. He seemed refreshingly willing to talk with me, though I am very much his senior. As we strolled on the wintry campus of an East Coast university, he shared some details of his past. His relationship with his parents, especially his father, had been distant when he was growing up. As a young teenager he had been sexually abused by an older man he trusted. This left him confused about his sexuality and wary of dependence. Following his parents' divorce during his late teens, his father, a college professor had taken up with a bisexual male companion, while his mother, nurturing her four children as best she could, had become an outspoken religious skeptic.

Despite these negative influences, Justin seemed to have experienced significant healing and to be growing into a sturdy, committed Christian. After telling his painful story, he began to share some aspects of his prayer and worship life. I put the question to him directly: "Given your troubled relationship with your father, Justin, have you found any difficulty praying to God as *Father*?" I assumed the answer would be yes. But Justin, frank as always, replied, "Absolutely not! For me the scriptural language about God as Father still rings powerfully true."

"Our Father"

The image of God as Father is deeply embedded in the Scriptures. In the Old Testament God's fatherhood is primarily an expression of His covenant, corporate relationship with the people of Israel (Ex. 4:22, 23; Ps. 103:13; Mal. 1:6; 3:17). Israel is "my son." The people are "His people;" He is

"their God." But in the New Testament God's fatherhood is both corporate and individual. The twelve
disciples, hearing Jesus use the intimate term
Abba, Father to describe the one with whom He com-
muned, could never forget it. Even when they
penned the Gospels, they did not attempt to trans-
late the phrase from the conversational Hebrew
Jesus used into Greek (Mark 14:36; see also Rom.
8:15; Gal. 4:6).

Jesus' use of the title *son* to refer to Himself—both
in the synoptic Gospels and especially in John—
showed how rooted was the idea of God's fatherhood in His own mind (Matt. 11:27; Luke 10:22; 22:70;
John 3:35; 5:20, 22; 17:1). He wanted the understanding rooted in the disciples' minds too, so He taught
them to pray to "Our Father" (Matt. 6:9–13). He told
them a story about God the Father who waits patiently for His lost son to return (Luke 15:11–32).
He assured them that His Father would give them
whatever they needed (Matt. 6:25–34). He taught
that His Father's pleasure was to give them the
kingdom (Matt. 7:11; Luke 12:32). He insisted that
He must be about His Father's business (Luke 2:49).
After His resurrection, He sent the eleven out to
preach and to baptize in the name of the "Father,
the Son, and the Holy Spirit." Of His imminent ascension Jesus said, "I am ascending to My Father
and your Father, and to My God and your God (John
20:17). There are in fact some 189 references to God
as Father in the Gospels, 65 of them outside the
Gospel of John, in which sonship is a favorite
theme.

Not surprisingly, Paul and the other apostles made this theme of fatherhood central to their proclamation of the good news: God has adopted us through faith into His family and sent His Spirit within us. Hence we may call Him Father. As a sign of His love for us, God disciplines us as a Father; and like a Father He showers His gifts upon us (Gal. 4:5; Rom. 8:14, 16; Heb. 12:7–9; Eph. 1:3).

The Earth Mother?

In our gender-conscious society this abundant scriptural testimony is viewed with suspicion. The idea of God as Father is criticized as the product of a male-dominated society, citing feminine images of God in the Bible. For example, in Isaiah 66:13, the Lord says "As one whom his mother comforts, so I will comfort you." Wisdom, *sophia*, one personification of God in the Old Testament, is a feminine noun (Prov. 1:20; 8:1; 9:1; see also The Wisdom of Solomon in the Apocrypha 7:24–26; 9:1). The Holy Spirit is feminine, some theologians propose, despite the fact that *ruach*, the word for spirit in Hebrew, while admittedly feminine in grammatical gender, is always masculine when used in the context of God. "When Spirit is personified to mean Spirit of the Lord, the accompanying pronouns and possessive adjectives are consistently masculine," says Donald Bloesch.[2] We cannot escape the overwhelming witness of Scripture that God chose to reveal Himself primarily through masculine imagery. While this imagery never means that God is male, the consistent witness does imply that God thought male imagery more especially appropriate to his self-revelation in history than female imagery.

Goddess religion is not a new idea. To the contrary, for millennia, from Canaanite religion in the Old Testament period to the mysteries of the New Testament era, goddess spirituality was dominant in pagan cultures. Earth Mother has been a perennial consort to Sky Father in religious thinking. But today, radical feminists want to *replace* the Sky Father with the Earth Mother because they believe that an immanent, rather than a transcendent, image of God would improve relations between the sexes in society.[3] Yet it was in Hebrew society, not in the pagan societies surrounding it, that women

---

Human-centered religion ultimately leads to the "paganization" of God.

---

were held in high esteem. Societies with female deities did not necessarily grant women special dignity. On the contrary, they were often held in low esteem, relegated to a purely sexual role.[4] There is an inherent logic to this: in the pagan paradigm of mated deities, creation comes out of the Earth Mother's fecundity. Therefore, modern ideas of the dignity of women—apart from their roles of sexuality and fertility—could not emerge in such societies.

The question for Christians then is not "How

should we change the image and language of the fatherhood of God?" but rather "How are we to understand it and see its relevance for today?" Can we confess the words "I believe in God the Father almighty, maker of heaven and earth"—words based on the Bible and used in the church as a baptism covenant for nearly two thousand years—*ex animo*, from the heart?

The Human-Centered Universe

Much of an understanding of the fatherhood of God depends on cultural assumptions. Although we are often unaware of them, assumptions affect the way we see issues and the outcome of our thinking more than we care to admit.

Beginning, as many do today, with the assumption that humankind is at the center of the universe, religion becomes but one aspect of anthropology. That is, religion is simply a part of the human story. The existence and nature of God (be God *he, she,* or *it*) is peripheral to the main story of the human adventure in all its wonder and mystery. Therefore, the Bible is to be treated as a quarry of inspiring ideas; perhaps it is even valuable as an instruction manual for morals and values. But it is clearly not what it purports to be: revelation from God. Human-centered religion ultimately leads to the "paganization" of God. God is granted a place in the cosmos; but humans are able to control God for their own purposes. By refusing to place God at the very center, the pagan mind rejects the divine authority so essential to true worship (Rom. 1:19–23).

The modern pagan mind, while willing to accept a God of love or a God of distant power, will not accept the union of authority and love in one being. This is reflected in the modern attitude toward human fatherhood. Fathers were once both loved as providers and defenders, and at the same time feared as disciplinarians. But as Harry Blamires says, in modern culture there is an "iron curtain" between authority and love.[5] Authority, now vested in the state, has become politicized and is viewed with suspicion. Love has been romanticized and is viewed with sentimentality.

One consequence of this severance of authority from love is the thinking that love justifies anything and authority justifies nothing. In terms of pop culture this plays out in an increasing tendency to lampoon human fatherhood. The modern British father is caricatured as follows:

> In reposeful moments [he] can be the best of company; at awkward moments he fumbles and exasperates. He is the poor fish who pays for unauthorized purchases by (his) wilful and frivolous womenfolk. He loses his pipe, forgets his umbrella, drops parcels in the street, and bursts the buttons from his braces. His highest delights are provided by the sporting pages of the daily *Press;* his familiar misfortune is the lawn-mower; his bitterest agonies are associated with the income tax.[6]

The characterization of the North American father brings its own unique contribution of racism, bigotry, and ineptitude. Consider Archie Bunker, Fred Flintstone, George Jefferson, and Dr. Cliff Huxtable and a father emerges who is humorous, bumbling, quixotic, and slightly pathetic. He exudes powerlessness, touchiness, shame, and despair, and his chronic absence, says Robert Bly, the founder of the modern "men's movement," is at the root of his children's many addictions.[7] Who really wants to hang around the house with such a person? No wonder there is not only humor directed at the modern dad, but also rage. And the spiral continues: with such rage and ridicule to contend with, why would father want to stay?

The Universe of the Generic God

Not everyone who rejects the fatherhood of God rejects a God-centered view of the world. Some believe the ideological watershed in society is the gulf between God and atheism, but the word *God* can be defined a number of ways. Room must be made for insights from all the great world religions. The idea of God goes beyond the words *him* or *her* or *it*. Creeds may point to that which is absolute, but at best they are only finite efforts to grasp the infinite. For example, the AIDS Awareness Committee of the Diocese of Toronto recently issued a series of litanies to be used in churches. One began: "Creator of the world; Our God, Allah, The Compassionate One, Wisdom, Spirit: We call you by many names for you have made us many people."[8]

To such thinkers the Bible is more than a mere

quarry of inspiring ideas; it is the record of a people's faith. It therefore deserves a revered place in the library of Great Thoughts. However, the Bible's ways of speaking about God should not be binding for cultures far removed from ancient Palestine. *God* is a generic term, rather than a personal name. It refers to that which is beyond names and adjectives and therefore is beyond all definition. Thus, again authority and love are sundered, for such a God has not revealed Himself adequately for us to know if He really loves *us* (and is personal) or has a specific will that we *must* obey (and is authoritative).[9]

The Christ-Centered Universe

Biblically-based creeds are based on a different assumption, the same as the Bible itself. Neither man-centered nor based on an abstract idea of God, the Bible and the historical creeds are Christ-centered. Both take as their starting point the fact that Jesus Christ, the incarnate Son of God, is the starting, ending, and focal point in the human story. Unless we understand that, we simply miss the point of it all.

Some, ignorant of the New Testament evidence itself, will ask, "But did Jesus really say about Himself that He was the Son of God?" In saying "Before Abraham was, I AM," Jesus was claiming that the whole of Jewish history pointed toward Him and was fulfilled in Him. He meant that the God whom the Jews worshiped as Yahweh was now fully revealed in Him (John 8:58). All the promises of the

Old Testament found fulfillment in His person and ministry. He was the "end," the consummation of the Law, as Paul put it (2 Cor. 1:20; Rom. 10:4).

It was not enough for Jesus that people be God-centered. If people were truly God-centered, He said, they would believe in Him as the only Son of God because the likeness between what he was saying and doing and what God had said and done was self-evident (John 5:36). But the religious leaders of the day—who were both God-centered and unable to deny the goodness of His actions—were unwilling to take this further step. Their only alternative was to crucify Him on a charge of blasphemy. In the decades to come, the apostles, refusing to yield to persistent and painful opposition, continued to proclaim the centrality of Christ as the only Son of the Father.

Authority and Love

Proceeding, then, with this assumption of the centrality of Jesus Christ, what was the distinguishing mark of His attitude toward the one he called Father? We discover it to be submission! Jesus desired only what the Father gave (Matt. 11:27). He would be about only His Father's business (Luke 2:49). He sought not His own will, but only that of His Father (John 5:30). He would teach only what the Father revealed to Him (John 8:28). He was not in control, the Father was. He was merely the vine; His Father was the vinedresser (John 15:1). When faced with the ultimate test, He cried out, "O My Father, if it is possible, let this cup pass from Me; nevertheless, not as I will, but as You will" (Matt. 26:39).

To Jesus, there was no question about the authority or power of the one He called Father. The Father's will was absolute, His purposes binding, His Word to be obeyed at all costs. The Father was God Almighty.

In a further reading of the Gospels a unique feature of this Almighty Father appears. He is not at all the stern, unapproachable Father we might suppose Him to be if He were merely a reflection of first century Palestinian culture. Far from being distant, Jesus' Father could be approached on the most intimate terms. *Abba,* which can be translated "Dear Father" or even, according to some, "Daddy" or "Papa," was how Jesus addressed Him in prayer. This Father is capable of tender emotion, even under difficult circumstances. As Jesus describes Him in the parable of the prodigal son, He treats both sons with great sensitivity. He waits painfully and patiently one's return from the far country and then in compassion runs, embraces, and kisses. The other son, afflicted with envy, pride, and stubbornness, He handles equally gently (Luke 15:11–32). Jesus is teaching us that God is a Father who cares intimately, provides generously, and deals patiently with His children (Matt. 6:25–34). God is supremely forgiving. No frightening heavenly policeman, God makes His covenant love known to us through the Cross, as we are enabled to see it by the Holy Spirit (Matt. 26:26–29; Rom. 5:5).

The Apostles' Creed builds upon this christological view of God's fatherhood. It is not "God in general" whom we confess in the Creed; it is the God and Father of our Lord Jesus Christ: the God of the covenant, of the Cross, the God who waits for errant children to return, the God who provides lovingly for His people, and the God whose Spirit enables us to call Him "Abba, Father."

A Bold Juxtaposition of Ideas

The Greek and Latin versions of the Apostles' Creed illustrate this combination of power and love in various ways. The Greek version of the Apostles' Creed uses *pantokrator,* meaning *ruler of all things.* Translated "Almighty," the word signifies a personal God as the one who rules all. The Latin version of the Creed, however, uses the word *omnipotens* for Almighty, which means simply "all-powerful." Therefore, while the Latin adjective *omnipotens* invites philosophical speculation, the Greek word *pantokrator* drives us back to Scripture to discover who this God is that rules all.[10]

God is a Father who cares intimately, provides generously, and deals patiently with His children.

By the juxtaposition of the two words *Father* and *Almighty,* the Apostles' Creed reunites what today's culture divides: the unity of love and power, of authority and compassion in one person. With Christ as the interpreter of God's fatherhood, God's power is not demonstrated as arbitrary or capricious but linked to the deepest and most nurturing aspects of personal caring. Nor is love presented as sentimental and indulgent but joined with authority and holiness. Our response should be true worship, which includes submission, obedience, and intimacy.

Farewell to Father's Day?

What is there to say to those whose experience of human fatherhood has left wounds and scars? Their view of fatherhood must be drawn from God, the true Father, and not from their own experience. Paul wrote: "I bow my knees to the Father of our Lord Jesus Christ, from whom the whole family in heaven and earth is named" (Eph. 3:14, 15). He reminded us that God is not made in our image; we are made in His. Therefore, our earthly experiences of fatherhood, even when most near the ideal, are merely icons of God's fatherhood. In only the faintest of ways, in the fractured mirror of our humanity, do they reflect the Real. Theologically, we argue from grace to nature, rather than the other way around. All pure forms of earthly love do point beyond themselves to God's love; but God loved us first. As James Stalker said, "In the Divine Being there is something great and incomprehensible from which all these earthly fires have been kindled."[11]

If each of us had perfectly adequate images of

fatherhood drawn from our human fathers, the temptation to idolatry would be great. The focus would be on human fathers rather than on God. Their very imperfection (which nevertheless is no excuse for inadequate fathering) is part of a creation subjected by God to futility, so that we might place our hope in that which is beyond the realm of sight (Rom. 8:20, 24). For this reason a succession of father images is needful in life: coaches, Boy Scout leaders, uncles, older friends, pastors, teachers, and so on. Each of these relationships, inadequate by itself, will contain some hint of that unique combination of authority and love found only in God.

What is to be said to the Freudians who postulate that out of disappointment with human fathers is fabricated the idea of a heavenly Father? This clever idea is no more plausible than the counterargument: Freudians reject the heavenly Father because they can't deal with the idea of a father at all. Why should we be unwilling to believe there is a correlation between our needs and reality? Is this not one more sign of a universe created by a master designer?

God-Talk

The effort to rework liturgical language and to replace masculine imagery for God with inclusive language in the Scriptures must be reviewed. God is not a limited male being; and there are feminine images for God in Scripture. But we must resist all intrusions from the naturalistic, mystic traditions of goddess spirituality. Jesus Christ has defined the nature and character of God as Father, once and for all. "We call God Father rather than Mother or neuter Parent because we believe that God himself has told us how to speak of him."[12]

This revelation does not negate the feminine but forbids locating a female within the trinity of Father, Son, and Holy Spirit. God as "Mother" would require a consort; such thinking goes back to the very paganism which Israel was commanded to forsake. God did not fully reveal His fatherhood until the incarnation ("born of a virgin"), for God did not need anything from the chosen woman other than her holiness of submission.

The sole feminine image found in the divine equation is the church, the bride of Christ. Luther, Calvin, and the Anabaptists affirmed the church as "mother," bearing the glory of God within its embrace as the dwelling of the Holy Spirit. "The divine fatherhood includes the divine motherhood ... [since] the motherhood of God is mirrored in the church."[13]

Seeing the Invisible

Confessing our faith in "God the Father almighty" defines fatherhood as it should be experienced here on earth. We fathers must ask how well we demonstrate to our children the qualities of fatherhood that Jesus revealed in God. Do we, in contrast to our culture, model that combination of authority and love, power and understanding, control and compassion that can be seen in and through Jesus Christ? The question which ought to exercise us is not: Why aren't our children submitting to us, but if they did submit, what would they see? Would they be brought closer to or driven further from Christ?

**God as "Mother" would
require a consort.**

Across the lounge in Denver's Stapleton Airport I spotted a family consisting of mother, father, and three active children. The two boys were probably 10 and 12, and I could see that they were getting very tired as they waited to say good-bye to Dad. Then things got out of hand. One of the boys must have done something to the other. I watched with growing interest as the father took each son aside for a brief but very firm talk. Being too far away to hear, I was able only to observe body language and facial expressions. But I noticed something unique in the combination of firmness and gentleness that came across in the way the father was treating his boys. I asked myself, is that man a Christian?

Not long afterward, my flight was called and I boarded a plane for Portland. To my surprise I discovered the man I had been watching had been assigned the seat next to me. In the course of the flight we talked extensively and I discovered that indeed he was a strongly committed Christian. Since then I have often remembered how, without a word, that man managed to communicate a healthy image of fatherhood, one that spoke eloquently of a deeper love and reality.

Questions for Discussion

1. How do you react to the pressure to exchange the names of God in the Bible and in worship for more "inclusive" terms? What fundamental theological issue is at stake in such changes?

2. Why should Jesus' view of God the Father be normative for us? How did His view differ from that of His own culture?

3. Do our parents' expectations color the way we view God's expectations of us? How ought the two to differ?

4. Where have you encountered a combination of authority and love? In coming to faith, how was such a combination helpful?

5. In what sense is the church an adequate image of motherhood for you?

Man Without Parallel

Jesus Christ his only Son our Lord

Seated around the attractive living room in Toronto's upscale neighborhood of Rosedale were some of the city's youngest and most successful entrepreneurs. A rising developer, the founder of a trendy fast-food chain, a dealer in fine leather goods, a lawyer, and others had come together with their spouses to hash out just what Liz and John's newfound faith really meant. Curried chicken, wild rice, spinach soufflé, and rich chocolate cake were only a prelude to the heavy discussion to come. Until coffee was served, conversation stayed superficial: the Blue Jays' chances for the World Series, downward signals in the economy, Liz's latest technique for making fireplaces look like marble, and of course babies and children. My wife Sandra and

I, sensing a challenging evening to come, had prepared ourselves in prayer for what we knew would be the first encounter many of these yuppies had had with "professional Christians."

"Isn't it time we got started?" asked Lynne. Her husband had been the one to suggest the gathering after the group had experienced a vigorous religious argument the previous summer at their favorite watering hole in the Muskoka Lakes. As Liz and John's rector, and a primary support in the new life of faith to which they had committed themselves only months before, I was on the hot seat. Neil was the first on his feet with a barrage of criticisms of Christianity, reminiscent of the arguments of hundreds of skeptical prep school students I had listened to during twenty-five years of ministry in America's independent schools.

Others soon joined in the discussion, which continued animatedly for nearly two hours. It appeared that these articulate, successful young Torontonians had never heard a defense of basic Christian doctrine. At the heart of their objections lay the central Christian claim that in Jesus Christ God became man, and that through faith in Him we could experience forgiveness and receive the gift of eternal life. The sheer generosity of this offer ran right up against their own deep-seated desire to earn the blessings of life the hard way: by working for them. After all, that was how most of them had arrived at their present status, so envied by their peers. Why would God want to change the rules of the game—especially when it appeared they were winning!

Neil, speaking for the rest, demanded an answer. "Why can't I be a Christian without going to church and believing in Jesus Christ?"

"Because the essence of being a Christian is believing in Jesus Christ," I replied.

This explanation left him unsatisfied, even after I sketched some of the reasons why Jesus was without parallel among human beings and why Christians believe that He is the Son of God. Finally, the real issue became clear. Neil wanted the respect that went with the designation *Christian,* for the label still counted for something in conservative Toronto despite the city's increasingly cosmopolitan population. But he could not bring himself to affirm, "Jesus is Lord."

"Well, Neil," I said, "no one is saying you can't be a good person without believing in Christ. You just can't legitimately claim the designation *Christian.*"

A quiet settled on the gathering, and people reached awkwardly for their coffee cups to cover up the silence. Then Adrienne turned to Liz and John and asked: "Tell us, now, what this new commitment of yours really means in your daily lives." With that, the confrontational atmosphere vanished as these two young believers struggled for words to express what coming to know Christ as human and as divine Lord meant to them.

The evening was over, and the late model autos spirited their owners home to more late-night conversation. But a seed had been planted. John soon started a men's breakfast group downtown to help friends discover God in the marketplace. Liz started a young moms' Bible study, fitting it in her busy life as a mother of three and a professional artist. The impact of their witness is still being felt.

The Heart of the Matter

Nothing is more central to Christian faith than the simple confession: "Jesus is Lord." It was the earliest Christian confession, and it lies at the heart of all the creeds (1 Cor. 12:3). No one can read the New Testament without realizing the theme undergirds the thought of every writer there. It is the unifying factor in the worldwide Christian movement, drawing people together from different cultures, races, and social and educational levels. Brilliant scholars and illiterates confess it. Martyrs have preferred to be burned at the stake or torn apart in the jaws of wild animals rather than deny it. Yet many, including those who consider themselves religious, are still offended by it. They know that if Christ is absolute Lord, then all other claims to divinity must be false.

Without this confession, the hope of salvation is cast into serious doubt. Paul said: "If you confess with your mouth the Lord Jesus and believe in your heart that God has raised Him from the dead, you will be saved. For with the heart one believes unto righteousness, and with the mouth confession is made unto salvation" (Rom. 10:9, 10).

No other religion puts such a premium on a personal confession of faith in its founder. Confucians, Muslims, Buddhists, and most other religious groups would be horrified at the thought of devotees making an exclusive claim for their founder. Furthermore, to the founders themselves, the idea that their followers would worship them, pray to them, and confess them as divine would have been anathema.

If Christ is absolute Lord, then all other claims to divinity must be false.

Yet Jesus, humble, self-effacing, and meek to a degree that even his enemies could not deny, permitted—even encouraged—people to fall at His feet, to praise Him, to hail Him as Master, and to see Him as the embodiment of God Himself (Matt. 11:29; 28:9; Luke 8:28; John 5:18; 8:46). This paradox has confounded opponents for two thousand years.

In the nineteenth century William Hazlitt, a British essayist and critic, wrote a famous piece titled, "Of Persons One Would Wish To Have Seen." Poets and other literati discuss great figures of the past, and then Hazlitt ends with these words: "If Shakespeare was to come into the room, we should all rise up to meet him. [But] there is one other Person . . . if that Person were to come into it, we should all fall down and try to kiss the hem of his garment." Hazlitt, of course, meant Jesus Christ.[1]

Many today would say that this nineteenth century piety no longer fits the modern age. But the late British journalist and former editor of *Punch*, Malcolm Muggeridge, who was converted to Christ after years of skepticism, thought that Christian belief had an internal logic to it.

> As far as Incarnation is concerned, I believe firmly in it . . . Eternity steps into Time, and Time loses itself in Eternity. Hence Jesus; in the eyes of God, a Man, and, in the eyes of men, a God. It is sublimely simple; a transcendental soap opera going on century after century in which there have been endless variations in the script, in the music, in the dialogue, but in which one thing remains constant— the central figure, Jesus.[2]

The Meaning of Faith

The word "believe," as used in the Bible, goes beyond intellectual assent to the idea of trust. James, in his epistle, contrasts the two: "You believe that there is one God. You do well. Even the demons believe—and tremble" (2:19). To James, such mere assent is light years from real faith.

The words *belief* and *believe* also include the sentiment of love. The Anglo-Saxon words *lief* and *luf* (love) are etymologically linked. Hence "to believe" is not just to permit or "give leave"; it is "to belove." To believe is to take into the heart, to adopt, to feel akin to or morally related to.[3]

There is, then, a risk in faith, just as there is a risk in trust and love. Contrary to the popular misconception that faith is "believing in your heart what you know in your head isn't so," biblical faith is not risk in spite of evidence, but rather, risk in scorn of consequence. It is, as Walter Trobisch says, like jumping. "I am pushed by logic, and pulled by One who longs to catch me."[4] Or, as Karl Barth said, just after he was suspended from his professorship for refusing to take the Hitler oath, "True trust in God begins where everything else ends."[5]

To confess faith in Jesus Christ is to have a personal relationship with Him. It is to know Him as the only way of salvation. It is to rely on Him in simplicity and with singleness of heart. It is to surrender the will. Until that point, what we call faith is what Barth called "little faith," which he likened to "little confessing" and "little repentance," and which he thought was worth, well, very little.

Emphatically Human

By including the name Jesus in the Creed we acknowledge faith in a historical man who was fully and emphatically human. It is hard for us, in our twentieth century culture, to understand why the humanity of Jesus was so controversial in the early centuries of the church. But then, as now, Christians were more influenced by the culture around them than they realized. A pervasive belief was that matter and spirit were irreconcilable opposites. Christians wondered how, if Christ was divine, His humanity could have been real? Wasn't this merely an illusion?

It wasn't long before widespread doubt took the form of heresy, with a ripple effect that continues even today. Docetism came from the Greek verb *dokein,* meaning "to seem," and denied the incarnation. Instead, the "Christ-spirit" must have come upon the man Jesus at baptism and departed before the crucifixion. Some, recoiling from the thought of God being crucified, went so far as to suggest that it was really Simon of Cyrene who was crucified, while Jesus looked on from a safe distance! This is likely what is behind the statement in the Koran (4:157) that the Jews did not kill Jesus, nor crucify Him, but "it was made ambiguous (or a semblance) to them."[6] The gospel of John and the Johannine epistles underscored the flesh and blood nature of the Son of God in part to counteract the widespread growth of Docetism (John 1:14; 19:34f.; 1 John 2:22f.; 4:2f.; 2 John 7).

Despite official condemnation by the early church, Docetism has proven remarkably resilient. It can still be found today in various forms: wherever spirituality is removed from the mundane events of life; or wherever orthodoxy, overreacting to the anti-supernatural bias of the times, stresses Jesus' divinity over against His humanity. As Sir Norman Anderson of Great Britain writes, concerning his evangelical heritage: "I look back on my youth and early middle age, [and] I am conscious that I thought of Jesus in such a way that his humanity was very largely swallowed up in his deity."[7]

Earthing the Truth

The belief that Jesus was fully human as well as the Son of God is not simply a test of Christian orthodoxy. It has very broad implications for the Christian view of the world. Allied with a belief in the humanity of Christ are some of the most cherished Christian convictions:

History Is Important

To say that Christianity is a historical religion doesn't mean that it belongs to the historians or simply started during an identified historical period. In the words of J. V. Langmead Casserley, Christianity "is the religion that compels [us] to make historical affirmations on the ground of faith."[8] When God became man, He affirmed that human events are important, that history is "His" story. Salvation is, therefore, not deliverance *from* history, as the Hindus see it, but deliverance *in* history.

Our Bodies Are Good

Our bodies, created by God and indwelt by the Holy Spirit, are the only visible "temples" God has today. Caring for them is therefore an ethical obligation. Indulging them carelessly or neglecting them thoughtlessly is wrong (1 Cor. 6:19).

Love Is Practical

Despite the unceasing efforts of Hollywood, Christians refuse to think of love as merely a feeling or an attraction. Love is incarnational. It is primarily a verb, rather than a noun. Love is unselfish action aimed at another person's well-being. It includes, among other things, a compassion for those who are needy and hurting. It builds hospitals and leprosy centers, sends doctors and dispenses medicines in Third World countries, takes meals to shut-ins, opens homes for unwed mothers, visits prisoners and lobbies for prison reform, builds housing for the poor, and so much more. "I am not claiming that all Christians at all times have given their lives in such service. But a sufficiently large number have done so to make their record noteworthy," says John Stott.[9]

Suffering Can Be Positive

Although suffering is in itself a negative, it can also be a force for creative moral, spiritual, and even physical change. It can wean us from an infantile reliance upon pleasure as the *summum bonum* of life. It can help bring back into focus neglected or discarded aspects of life. History's honor roll is filled with people who embraced suffering for the sake of others. For example, Dr. Jesse W. Lazier, while collecting blood from yellow fever patients, noticed a mosquito on the back of his hand. At the time it was widely thought, though not yet proven, that the deadly virus was passed from human to human via the female *aedes aegypti* mosquito. Dr. Lazier decided to allow the insect to stay on his hand until it had drunk its fill. Months later he died of yellow fever, with these words on his lips: "For twenty years my prayer has been that I might be permitted in some way or at some time to do something to alleviate human suffering." Lazier's sacrifice became the proof the scientific community sought.

**_Love_ is primarily a verb,
rather than a noun.**

Would we hold to these convictions had God remained aloof from the human condition? The name _Jesus_ literally means "God to the rescue." God, becoming a historical human being, dwelling in a flesh-and-blood body, demonstrating love in practical ways, and enduring suffering for the good of others, forged the link to effect the rescue we so desperately needed.

Confessing Jesus as the Christ means that I believe in a God who has shared all the limitations and struggles of a human body with me. God knew what it was to be tired, dirty, hungry, and thirsty. God knew what it was to be in pain, even to endure the abyss of death. God knew loneliness, fear, temptation, anger, rejection, weakness, tenderness, joy, and excitement. God shared a human environment with us, caring for society, weeping over Jerusalem, railing against injustice, challenging corruption, healing the sick, and feeding the multitudes. As Kierkegaard said: His life ran like ours "from womb to tomb."

Decisively Divine

We must begin with the humanity of Jesus because it is usually through His humanity that people come to see His divinity. As Luther said, "The Scriptures begin very gently, and lead us on to Christ as to a man, and then to one who is Lord over all creatures, and after that to one who is God." To begin with abstracts, as the philosophers and academic theologians do, said Luther, is a sure way of never coming to the knowledge of God.[10]

The step from the humanity to the divinity of Christ is one the average person finds difficult. An important shift in world view has taken place in the last fifty years. The main obstacle to people accepting the divinity of Jesus is rarely, as it used to be, the miraculous nature of many of his actions. The borders of science have expanded such that indeterminacy and relativity permit the mysterious and condone the miraculous. The main obstacles to belief in the divinity of *Jesus* come from New Age notions that man is God; then the pantheist idea that, since humans are part of the divine cosmos, the divinity of one can be no different from the divinity of all; and, allied with these, the relativist insistence that no one historical event can be normative for all people in all times.[11]

The centrality of the divinity of Christ was driven home recently when, at the request of a friend, I visited a stranger dying of cancer in Toronto's Falk Clinic. Although the patient was an Episcopalian, his wife and brother-in-law were Roman Catholics. They were in the room with him when I arrived. As we talked, there seemed to be an unspoken reservation about my theology, but I reasoned that, since they didn't know me and I was not a priest in their church, it was quite natural. At the close of the visit I offered a simple prayer for the dying man and for the members of his family. At the conclusion the brother-in-law said quietly: "Jesus Christ, true Son of Man, true Son of God." I sensed that he was probing for a response, so I smiled and said: "He certainly is!" The confession was the key that unlocked the door. Instantly, we knew that we were brothers.

But would every clergyman of my denomination be able to answer so decisively? The sad fact is that while many long-time churchgoers assume that belief in the divinity of Jesus Christ automatically goes with the title *Reverend,* there is profound debate within the church on this very subject. At a recent convention of the Episcopal Diocese of Pennsylvania the following resolution was defeated:

> That we "do believe the Holy Scriptures of the Old and New Testaments to be the Word of God, and to contain all things necessary to salvation" (*Book of Common Prayer,* p. 526) and that we do believe, in accordance with the same Scriptures and our Anglican tradition, that "Jesus is the Christ, the only name under heaven by which we may be saved." (Acts 4:12, Article XVII of the Articles of Religion.)

Of the 142 clergy who voted, only 57 were in favor! Of the 144 laity who voted, only 67 said yes. Yet could there have been a more simple, direct reaffirmation of Christ and the Scriptures?

Eternally Yours

The New Testament proclaims the full divinity of Jesus.[12] The early church father Origen (A.D. 185–254) spelled out the implications of this with his doctrine of the "eternal generation" of the Son. That is, the Father did not "create" the Son; the Son was begotten or generated from the very being of God from all eternity.[13] At no point in His life was Jesus made the Son of God; He was eternally the Son. When He acted, it was God in action. When He loved, it was God loving. When He spoke, it was God speaking. When He mended and transformed lives, it was God's power at work (see John 5:17).

It is quite inadequate to say, as the ancient heretic Arius (A.D. c. 250–336) and his modern day followers claim, that Jesus was merely like God.[14] Jesus never said that. In fact, the record states that He said the reverse: God was like Him (see Matt. 11:28; John 14:9).

Mistaken Identity?

Consider the problems if Jesus Christ is not fully God. First is the issue of revelation. Would there be assurance that the God Jesus claimed to reveal was the real God? After all, asked Jesus, has anyone ever ascended into heaven to find out what God is like? (John 3:13). Only if someone descended from the Father could we be enlightened.[15]

Another problem is salvation. Would there be assurance that we can be free from the guilt of sin without a savior who is fully divine and capable of guaranteeing God's unconditional forgiveness? Redemption, which is both a present release from the guilt of sin and a future release from its power, depends on the action of God reaching out to us in our need. Human experience teaches that the initiative for forgiveness must always come from the one who has been grieved.

Unless Jesus Christ is fully divine, He cannot be accessible to us now.

Lastly, there is the problem of growing in Christ. How is growth in spiritual maturity possible without regular, personal, intimate contact with Him? How is that contact possible if He is long ago and far away? Jesus said that unless we eat His flesh and drink His blood we have no "life" within us (John 6:53). He also said that He was the "bread of life" (John 6:35). Clearly, unless Jesus Christ is fully divine, He cannot be accessible to us now. His presence is mediated to us through the means of grace available—the Word of God read, proclaimed, dramatized in Holy Communion, and lived out in the fellowship of believers. Here we are fed with nothing less than the living Christ Himself. Isn't the ongoing benefit of these vital channels drastically reduced if they only remind us of a God who once loved us?

Feodor Dostoevsky, one of the greatest Russian novelists, saw the centrality of Christ. He said, "The most pressing question on the problem of faith is whether a man, as a civilized being . . . can believe in the divinity of the Son of God, Jesus Christ, for therein rests the whole of our faith."[16]

The conviction is still held by many today. The December 23, 1990, edition of the *Moscow News,* an independent weekly, published the results of an opinion poll conducted by VCIOM, the Soviet Centre of Public Opinion and Market Research. The poll covered a wide range of issues. For instance, 44 percent of the more than 1,300 people surveyed in 21 localities believed that the USSR would begin to "disintegrate" within six months. Twenty-seven percent believed that mass famine would commence. Fifty-eight percent believed that a wave of strikes would begin. Then a curious question followed: "Which of the following names, in your opinion, will be of great importance to the peoples of the USSR in the year 2000?" The answers: Josef Stalin: 9 percent; Mikhail Gorbachev: 26 percent; Nikolai Lenin: 36 percent; Andrei Sakharov: 48 percent; Jesus Christ: 58 percent.

Metamorphosis

Some would give up faith in the divinity of Jesus for the sake of peace and unity with other religions.

Hugh Schonfield, the popular Jewish author and apologist, argues that it was under the impact of Gnosticism that Jesus Christ was converted from Son of God to God the Son. He pleads for the creation of a combined Jewish/Christian monotheistic faith in which Jews give up their Zionism and Christians give up their belief in the unique divinity of Jesus.[17] But what he (and some within the church who urge syncretism) overlook is that a belief in Jesus as God the Son is always the result of divine revelation. "Flesh and blood has not revealed this to you," said Jesus to Peter upon his confession of faith (Matt. 16:17).

A cursory reading of the Gospels reveals that, until the Spirit brought full conviction, even the disciples vacillated between bold, vigorous faith and weak, hesitant doubt. "Lord, I believe; help my unbelief!" is where many start in their journey toward that certainty which the Spirit gives (Mark 9:24).

One evening, in an effort to bolster their weak faith, Jesus took Peter, James, and John to the top of a high mountain. There, while the three struggled to stay awake following the tiring climb, Jesus entered into intense prayer. As he prayed, His face began to metamorphose. His tanned skin turned white and began to shine. His eyes blazed. The dusty wool robe He wore glistened in the moonlight with a dazzling luminosity. Then, as an eerie cloud enveloped them, the three men saw Moses and Elijah, patriarchal representatives of the Law and the Prophets, talking with Jesus about His coming death. Totally overwhelmed, the disciples camouflaged their fear with inane comments, such as "Wouldn't it be nice if we could just stay here a bit longer?"

Such naive enthusiasm could be overlooked, but one of Peter's comments drew a stern, heavenly rebuke. "Let us make three tabernacles here," he suggested when Jesus had emerged from the cloud. "One for You, one for Moses, and one for Elijah." From a human point of view, it was all quite understandable. Peter was trying to harmonize his reverence for Jesus with his reverence for Moses and the prophets, in the way those who are unwilling to draw distinctions want to elevate the founders of the world's various religions to the same status as that of Jesus. But God's answer was shatteringly abrupt. From the cloud came a voice that said: "This is My beloved Son. Hear Him!" No sooner had the voice been heard than Jesus reappeared in his original form—alone (see Luke 9:28–36).

Blaise Pascal, one of the greatest philosophers and scientists of the seventeenth century, discovered the uniqueness and glory of Jesus Christ through a sudden revelation, a record of which he kept on his person until his death. In a fragment of what would have been a much larger apologetic work, he wrote:

> Jesus Christ is the object of all things, the center upon which all things focus ... All those who seek God apart from Christ ... either find no light to satisfy them or find no way of knowing and serving God ... God's deity only exists through Christ and for Christ.[18]

Pascal knew that only a fully human Jesus reaches the depths of the human condition, but only a fully divine Jesus lifts us beyond those depths. Such a high christology, as it is called, will always offend some. However, a Jesus who never quite makes it either to the depths or the heights isn't really worth our consideration. The nineteenth century Danish philosopher Kierkegaard mocked the oft-heard reverence which hails Jesus as (merely) a great prophet or teacher: "It is blasphemous to have a heedless reverence for Him whom one must either believe in or be offended at."[19]

Questions for Discussion

1. Why do people confuse the words *Christian* and *good person?*

2. Why is the confession "Jesus is Lord" controversial?

3. In what sense is faith a risk?

4. How important is it to you that the Jesus of history and the Christ of faith are one and the same?

5. "If Christ were not divine, reading the Bible would be like reading letters from someone long dead." In what ways is the divinity of Christ essential for Christian nurture?

6. What is behind the syncretistic impulse that puts other religious founders on a level with Christ?

4

Second Adam
to the Rescue

Born of the Virgin Mary

Ten or twelve relatives—aunts, uncles, cousins—gathered around the generous mahogany dining room table in my grandparents' sturdy suburban home outside New York City. The decibel level of the conversation was, as usual, quite high, in part due to the poor hearing of my grandparents and in part due to the animated way the family carries on its intergenerational chatter. Such dinners were always fun, and the clink of glasses was usually accompanied by humorous storytelling. My grandmother was an admirable raconteur, and she always invited laughter because her stories were alternately either very good or very bad! However, now that she was in her mid-eighties, her arteries had begun to harden, and no one quite knew what words might come out of her mouth.

On this evening, my mother and I sat at opposite sides of the table, with my grandfather at one end, and my grandmother at the other. There was a lull in the conversation. My grandmother began to look pensively first at my mother, then at me, and then back at my mother. "Now, tell me," she said very deliberately, "when was it you two first met?"

Understandable Confusion

Her understandable confusion underscores the importance of asking the right questions when considering the virgin birth of Jesus Christ. The very question "Was Jesus born of a virgin?" sends us down the wrong road right away. The New Testament does not talk about a "virgin birth" at all; but rather a virginal conception. Our Lord was conceived without a human father.

Virginal conception, in turn, often is confused with the Roman Catholic doctrine of the Immaculate Conception proclaimed by the Catholic Church in 1854, which states that Mary was herself not only a virgin but also was conceived without sin. The Immaculate Conception is a logical extension of the belief that since Mary was the mother of Jesus and therefore the mother of God, it was not possible that she could have been an ordinary, sinful mortal. She must, therefore, have been sinless.

This has often led to a further belief about Mary. Since for many years sections of the church mistakenly taught that sex was inseparable from lust, the logical conclusion to devout souls was that if Mary was sinless at the conception of Jesus, she must have remained "pure" throughout the rest of her life. The doctrine was called the Perpetual Virginity of Mary, with its corollary that Jesus' brothers and sisters, mentioned in the New Testament (see Matt. 13:55, 56; Gal. 1:19), must have been children of Joseph by a former wife!

Using the same logic, devout Catholics came to believe that if Mary was sinless throughout her life, then she could not have died like other mortals. Her body must not have decomposed like the bodies of other mortals, but must have been immediately assumed into heaven. Hence the doctrine of the Bodily Assumption of Mary, promulgated by Pope Pius XII in 1950. It is important not to confuse any of these doctrines with the virgin birth (or, properly, the virginal conception) which alone has support within the Bible. On account of the lack of biblical support, the various marian doctrines mentioned remain an obstacle in ecumenical discussion.[1]

Lamentable Controversy

In addition to the confusion with non-scriptural doctrines about the Virgin Mary, Jesus' virgin birth has been a center of theological controversy, especially in recent times. Two examples illustrate this point. A young preacher in a respectable mainline pulpit announced his topic for the morning: the birth of Jesus Christ. With some skill he outlined the traditional doctrine as taught by Matthew and Luke, and as contained in the creeds. But he continued by saying that the doctrine of the virgin birth was inseparably linked with the church's historic stance against sexuality. Because this position represented a refusal to admit the goodness of creation and procreation, the doctrine of the virgin birth needed to be relegated, along with other outmoded ideas, to the ash heap of teachings that have stood in the way of a more enlightened understanding of the faith!

The second example comes from my own parish in Toronto, a historically evangelical congregation within the Anglican Church of Canada. Prior to my arrival as rector, a noted conservative theologian had preached a polemical sermon on the virgin birth with such vehemence and defensiveness that folk in the pews were profoundly disturbed. It appeared that many had doubts about this doctrine, even though they said the Apostles' Creed Sunday by Sunday. I decided to give them a questionnaire in order to learn just where they stood on a number of theological, ethical, and pastoral issues. Of the 200 respondents, 87 percent of them believed the virgin birth. Seven percent were undecided, and only 6 percent said that they had doubts. The conclusion: Many a doctrine is never doubted until someone tries too hard to defend it.

Unfortunately, modern controversies surrounding the virgin birth have tended to obscure the original reason for including this article in the Apostles'

Creed. At the time, the debate centered not on the first word, *virgin*, but on the second word, *birth*. Its inclusion in the Creed was intended to underscore the full humanity of Jesus for those who, in their zeal for a fully divine Jesus, rejected Him as having been fully human.[2] Ironically, people today invariably hear the accent fall on the first of the two words: *virgin* birth. In addition to the skepticism reserved for miracles, there is a rejection of the doctrine of the virgin birth on theological grounds.

====

Many a doctrine is never doubted until someone tries too hard to defend it.

====

Until Karl Barth surprised the scholarly world of the twentieth century with his defense of the virgin birth, liberals and conservatives had drawn the battle lines clearly. Conservatives made the virgin birth a test of orthodoxy. It has been included in virtually every conservative doctrinal statement of Protestant and evangelical organizations in this century. Liberals, on the other hand, have made a point of questioning it. People in the middle, like William Barclay, found the evidence for the virgin birth "inconclusive"; but pleaded for charity among those on either side of the fence.[3]

This issue is a theological minefield, where the danger of explosive reactions is ever present and vultures attend the outcome. "Conceived by the Holy Spirit, born of the Virgin Mary," says the Apostles' Creed. Is it necessary? Is it possible? Is it consistent?

The Issue of Necessity

Conservative scholars certainly have thought the virgin birth was necessary. In the early part of this century, Benjamin B. Warfield wrote:

> It [is] imperatively necessary that [Jesus] should become incarnate after a fashion which would leave him standing . . . outside that fatal entail of sin in which the whole natural race of Adam is involved. And that is as much as to say that the redemptive work of the Son of God depends upon his supernatural birth.[4]

But is it as necessary as Warfield thought? The sinlessness of Jesus can certainly be protected without it, since Scripture teaches that His sinlessness was something He earned throughout the entire course of his life, rather than something given as part of His nature. "He learned obedience by the things which He suffered," says the book of Hebrews (5:8); and the Gospels testify to His real struggle in resisting the devil's temptations in the wilderness (see Matt. 4:1–11). Another conservative scholar, W. H. Griffith Thomas, sought to distinguish between Jesus' character, which he said was an attainment, and His personality, which he said was an endowment. However, this effort to have your cake and eat it too fails to convince.[5]

Is belief in the virgin birth necessary to protect the Incarnation—the cardinal doctrine that God became man? Could God not have chosen to send His Son into the world through a normal process of conception and birth, had He wished? The virgin birth, of course, guarantees that Jesus was extraordinary, to say the least. On the basis of a closed system of cause and effect, parthenogenesis (birth without the sperm of a human male) is miraculous. Apologists from the earliest days of the church have not hesitated to use the virgin birth as a guarantee of Jesus' divinity.[6] But this does not establish that the virgin birth was necessary.

Anti-Christian apologists have used the story of the virgin birth to their advantage, too. Rumors circulated in the early years of the church that the real father of Mary's child was a Roman soldier named Ben Panthera, an idea which may have had roots in the early Jewish reaction to Jesus. "*We* were not born of fornication," said the Jews to Jesus in the midst of a heated controversy, as if to suggest that *He* were (John 8:41; italics mine).

Biblical Passages

Much is made of the fact that only Matthew and Luke report the virgin birth, and that neither Mark nor John refer to it in their gospels. Paul does not mention it, although he certainly knew of it: "When the fullness of the time had come, God sent forth His Son, born of a woman, born under the law" (Gal. 4:4). But why, people ask, if the virgin birth is necessary as part of belief in the Incarnation, do only two of at least nine New Testament writers mention it?

Some argue that biblical prophecy necessitates the virgin birth. But Matthew quotes only one Old Testament verse in support of it: Isaiah 7:14. "Behold, the virgin shall conceive and bear a Son, and shall call His name Immanuel." Scholars have rightly pointed out that the Hebrew word for *virgin* (*almah*) can just as easily be translated "young woman." Moreover, this prophecy was to announce the birth of an extraordinary child, presumably during the reign of King Ahaz. The child was to be a sign to Ahaz that the enemy he was then facing would soon be removed. It was certainly correct for Matthew to see the child as a symbol of Christ who is to come, for the name *Immanuel*, meaning "God with us," heralded more than a mere human offspring. But in its original context the prophecy referred to a local event in the time of Isaiah.

Therefore, the virgin birth is not necessary to belief in the Incarnation. Present confession functions as a safeguard of the integrity of the biblical record; and for those who doubt the virgin birth, the issue is then raised of the credibility of all the supernatural elements in the Bible. Yet why should this doctrine appear in the Apostles' Creed alongside such central truths as the Cross and the Resurrection?

The Issue of Possibility

Belief in the possibility of the virgin birth is contingent upon belief in miracle. This basic link cannot be avoided. If the universe is an interlocking system where no outside power can break the endless chain of cause and effect, then miracles are impossible. On this view, natural law prohibits anything "unnatural" from happening.

C. S. Lewis rightly pointed out, however, that placing the natural and the supernatural over against each other creates a false antithesis. "A miracle is emphatically not an event without a cause or without results. Its cause is the activity of God: its results follow according to Natural law." If people take Nature to be the whole of reality, Lewis argued, then everything must be related *both forward* in terms of results, *and backward* in terms of cause. But in miracles God creates a new situation which Nature immediately "domiciles." "If God creates a miraculous spermatozoan in the body of a virgin, it does not proceed to break any laws. The laws at once take it over. Nature is ready. Pregnancy follows, according to all the normal laws, and nine months later a child is born." Lewis sums up his point by saying that if God is the ultimate cause, He can also be the proximate cause: "The great complex event called Nature, and the new particular event introduced into it by the miracle, are related by their common origin in God."[7]

Many have found that naturalistic assumptions are inadequate to explain all that life and history present.[8] Nevertheless, some theologians seem prepared to reject the Resurrection, the Ascension, the miracles of Jesus—indeed the whole biblical testimony to miracles in both the Old and the New Testaments—because of a prior belief in a closed system of cause and effect. On these grounds Lewis argued that the Incarnation, the "Grand Miracle," must be demythologized. The whole structure of Christian belief must be reshaped to fit into a naturalistic world view.[9] As any student of theology knows well, many do not hesitate to do this. Indeed, they feel an obligation to rescue Christianity from obscurantism. Emil Brunner, to take just one example, saw belief in the virgin birth as a form of "little faith."[10]

Others see natural law as descriptive, rather than prescriptive. Natural laws describe how things usually happen, but they cannot limit what will or will not happen. Together with the whole of the universe, they are under God's ultimate control. God's sovereign discretion may be to suspend His usual way of doing things if He sees good reason to do so. Interestingly, in Luke's birth narrative God is mentioned no fewer than fifty-eight times, as if the author wishes to underscore the extraordinary nature of this one birth.

Contrary to what has been suggested, miracles in those days were not expected, everyday occurrences. In Matthew and Luke, it is clear that Mary and Joseph were surprised to learn of her unusual pregnancy. Why else would Joseph have made the decision to break their engagement? "Joseph knew just as well as any modern gynaecologist that in the ordinary course of nature women do not have babies unless they have lain with men," wrote C. S. Lewis. When Joseph finally accepted the message that Mary's pregnancy was due not to unchastity but to a miracle, he believed the baby's conception to be something at variance with the known order of nature and resolved not to have sexual relations with her until after the child was born.[11]

Natural laws describe how things usually happen, but they cannot limit what will or will not happen.

But is the virgin birth the real stumbling block to faith that many have made it out to be? As Donald Bloesch writes:

> Like the empty tomb [the virgin birth] is a sign that serves to communicate [the central mystery of faith]. It is not itself the stumbling block, but it is a potent witness to the real stumbling block of faith—the Son of God becoming man and taking upon himself the sin and guilt of mankind.[12]

Those who profess belief in the Incarnation but not the virgin birth rarely say unequivocally that in Jesus Christ "God became man." Instead, God is present "somehow" or "in some way" or "in a real way" in Christ. Does this mean that God was in Christ in the way that God is in all of us—only more so?

The Issue of Consistency

If the possibility of the virgin birth is true, is the virgin birth consistent with the overall revelation of Christ?

Some argue that the many ancient stories of gods mating with beautiful women indicate that a virginal birth is consistent with the overall mythical character of religion. The virgin birth, as with other miraculous elements in the gospel story, serves to demonstrate Christianity's unhistorical character. However, such pagan borrowings would have been inconceivable to the faithful Jewish/Christian mind; furthermore, never once did mythology suggest that these matings took place in time and space with a historical mother and baby.

Just as a nonhistorical view of the virgin birth should be avoided, so should too mundane a view. Jesus is God's Son, not in the sense that the Father provided the invisible seed that Mary needed so that conception took place via the womb. Matthew and Luke tell us that Mary heard the Word of God and said: "Let it be to me according to your word" (Luke 1:38). Life came to Mary as it always comes in Scripture, through the Word of God.

It is to Karl Barth that we owe gratitude for the most helpful modern insights on the virgin birth. Barth, undeniably one of the great theologians of this century, astonished the scholarly world by accepting the miracle of Christmas. For him the virgin birth was a miracle in the Johannine sense that all miracles are signs pointing to Christ. Barth said that the virgin birth did not prove the Incarnation but is entirely consistent with it.

Special Creation

Barth said that the miracle of Christmas pointed to Jesus' true origin as a special creation of God. Just as in Genesis God created "out of nothing," this time God created "of the Virgin Mary." Barth was impressed by the prominence of the Spirit in both Matthew's and Luke's birth narratives, reminding him of the beginning of time when the Spirit brooded over the creation bringing order and matter into existence.

Sovereign Action

The miracle of Christmas also illustrated to Barth the sovereignty of God because it spoke of intention and initiative. No human being decided to bring this child into the world. The decision was God's, His election, from start to finish. "The only love at work in the coming of God's Son is the love of the Father for the Son in the Holy Spirit."[13]

Earthward Direction

Third, the miracle of Christmas spoke to Barth of the direction of the Incarnation. Even though Jesus was both God and man, His birth was not the result of a fifty-fifty bargain in which God supplied part and humanity supplied the other part. God did not meet humanity halfway in the Incarnation. The direction of the Incarnation was decidedly and irreversibly from God to humanity, from heaven to earth, from the eternal into time. A sovereign God took the initiative and made Himself man, giving Himself an earthly, human origin in the Virgin Mary but acting as Creator, not partner with her. Barth concludes, "We cannot [say] that the reality of the Incarnation . . . had by necessity to take the form of this miracle . . . All that we can say is that it pleased God to let the mystery be real and become manifest in this shape and form."[14]

Sadly, coming to this doctrine many miss the forest for the trees. They look first at the component parts of the Christian faith and stumble at the Ascension, the Resurrection, the virgin birth, the feeding of the five thousand, the walking on water, and so on. They wrongly suppose that, until they believe all these details, they cannot accept the general thesis.

But consider how the first Christians approached these claims. They came to know Jesus Christ first of all as a living presence and power in their lives, delivering them from sin, freeing them to know and love God and empowering them to accept one another as brothers and sisters across racial and ethnic barriers. Then only after Christ had captured their hearts did they encounter the specifics. Of course, by then they had little difficulty seeing Jesus as utterly unique. The whole of the apostolic witness seemed entirely consistent with all that they knew to be true of Him. Similarly, we too must come to know Christ ourselves by the Holy Spirit before we tackle a doctrine like the virgin birth. Then what the Bible says to our mind God will already have said to our heart.

Novelist John Irving, whose many best-selling books often depict a brooding presence which seems to guide in some way the lives of his characters, has created a modern parable in *A Prayer for Owen Meany*. Owen, a short, intense, God-conscious young man driven by a sense of destiny, is handicapped socially by an unpleasantly high-pitched voice and by the poverty of his family upbringing. Nevertheless, his best friend is a wealthy New England private school boy, and it is through this friend's eyes that Irving's story is told. Outwitting opponents and detractors, Owen emerges from his teenage years to enlist in the army. During training to go to Vietnam he eventually meets a tragic end: He gives his life to save a group of refugee children from a terrorist's grenade.

Johnny Wheelwright, Owen's friend, struggling to understand the mysterious force which moved Owen to a sacrificial death, stumbles upon an amazing piece of information: At twelve Owen had been told by his parents that his had been a miraculous conception! "'You're saying that Owen was a virgin birth?' I asked Mr. Meany; he wouldn't look at me, but he nodded vigorously. 'She was a virgin—yes!' he said." Johnny, outraged, ponders how that story must have weighed heavily on Owen's mind. Angered and confused, he goes to the Rev. Lewis Merrill, the local Congregationalist minister, for whom he has little respect. "Owen Meany didn't exactly believe he was Jesus Christ," confesses Merrill, "but he said to me that if I could believe in one virgin birth, why not in another one?" Johnny, suspecting that Merrill's skepticism prevented him from believing in either, presses him to declare or deny his faith in Owen. With that the minister's attitude becomes condescending, and he advises Johnny not to confuse his grief with genuine religious belief. At that, Johnny explodes:

> You don't seem to me to believe very much in God— or in *any* of those so-called miracles. You're always talking about "doubt as the essence and not the opposite of faith"—but it seems to me that *your* doubt has taken control of you. I think that's what Owen thought about you too.[15]

Through the eyes of Johnny, a searching soul who vacillates between skepticism and belief, Irving creates in Owen a modern Christ-figure. His well-told tale is a parable—unintended perhaps—of the sign value of the virgin birth in the New Testament. Owen's vicarious death, his sense of "destiny," his God-consciousness combined with an intense humanity, all parallel (by no means exactly, of course) the picture we have of Jesus in the New Testament. When we discover that, at an impressionable age, Owen had been told of his "supernatural" birth we gain some insight into his drivenness. Similarly, on reading that Mary pondered all the details of her son's birth in her heart, we wonder what impact the knowledge of His remarkable birth might have had upon Jesus' later ministry (Luke 2:51). Certainly Mary shared with Him the stories which Matthew and Luke record. Would not this have deepened His consciousness that He was indeed a chosen vessel?

A Radical Challenge

The virgin birth can speak prophetically to contemporary life if we are able to get above and beyond the offense to modern scientific prejudice.

The female (though not the feminine) is excluded from our understanding of God the Father. Conversely, in the virgin birth, the male (though not the masculine) is excluded. In His sovereignty God chose to bypass the normal role of the male in the work of redemption. God has no problem with gender itself, or He would not have created both male and female in His image (see Gen. 1:27). But in the virgin birth God excluded the male to symbolize that aspect of humanity which, in its pride, sees itself as the prime shaper of civilization, as the Lord of creation. "This human being, this patriarch, this head of the family, this Mr. Fix-it—is by [the virgin birth]—unmistakably set aside."[16] God, needing no co-redemptor or co-redeemer, chose to involve humanity in only one way—in the figure of the virgin Mary. Man as a creating, controlling, self-assertive, self-glorifying being was set aside in favor of a woman who listened, received, and served.

Those in the church who have honored the Blessed Virgin have been right to do so and are on solid scriptural grounds. But God's sovereign choice of Mary also is a challenge to the human psychological need to contribute to our own salvation, to be co-creators with God. Mary stands as a witness against the drive, push, and self-assertion that men especially (though not exclusively) associate with a healthy self-image and by which men often mask their own impotence. The radical nature of her challenge is to be found in her song, the Magnificat. Mary sings that in the life of her Son, the mighty will be cast down from their seats and the humble and meek will be exalted (see Luke 1:52).

The first Adam sought the way of self-advancement. With his failure humanity set out on a long trek through the desert in search of the lost self. Each of us as part of that lost humanity has felt God's judgment in all the failed vanities the Bible calls sin. We know how fruitless and vain that quest has been. But God broke in in an extraordinary way. A second Adam, both God and man, appeared to reverse the sad, downward pull of sin, in which we all have participated. While it was not necessary that Jesus be born of a virgin, it was entirely consistent with God's plan. Jesus' unique conception is a sign to us of God's sovereign action, full of grace, on our behalf.

> O loving wisdom of our God!
> When all was sin and shame,
> A second Adam to the fight
> And to the rescue came.
>
> O wisest love! that flesh and blood
> Which did in Adam fail,
> Should strive afresh against the foe,
> Should strive and should prevail.[17]

Questions for Discussion

1. On what basis do you judge the various marian doctrines to be right or wrong?

2. Does seeing an immediate local fulfillment of Isaiah 7:14 preclude its long-term fulfillment in the birth of Jesus? Can prophecy have more than one fulfillment?

3. Why has belief in the virgin birth become a "test of orthodoxy"?

4. Do you agree with Donald Bloesch that the real stumbling block to faith is not the virgin birth but the incarnation and substitutionary death of Jesus?

5. How does the sovereignty of God, expressed in the sign of the virgin birth, deepen your understanding of salvation?

5

Dancing with the Devil on Your Back

Suffered, crucified, dead, buried, descended

Jesus could have chosen any week of the year to plan His entry into the holy city of Jerusalem, but He chose the week that coincided with the celebration of Passover. He knew that by doing so He would synchronize His death with the annual killing of the Passover lamb—that annual reminder of the blood which the Hebrew slaves in Egypt sprinkled over the lintels of their doors the eve of the Exodus to ensure that the angel of death would "pass over" them. By linking His death with this feast, Jesus ensured that it would forever be tied to the concept of sacrifice.

There was a tension about the fanfare surrounding Jesus when He approached the Golden Gates on the east side of the city that afternoon. The shouts of praise and the waving of palm fronds could not mask the growing antagonism from other quarters. Jesus' enemies were already angered by His expulsion of the money changers from the temple earlier that week, an act that threatened what they considered to be a legitimate enterprise. They found His manner of entering the city—on a donkey rather than a horse—to be conspicuously provocative: a deliberate ploy to make Jesus appear to be fulfilling the ancient prophecy of the Messiah's coming in humility, riding on an ass (see Zech. 9:9). In their minds, Jesus was inflaming the already widespread suspicion that He was the long-awaited deliverer. No wonder they strenuously objected to the whole event (see Matt. 21:10; John 12:19).

Redefinition of Joy

In the revised lectionaries now used in most churches that follow the liturgical calendar, the Sunday immediately before Easter has been changed from Palm Sunday to Passion Sunday. Readings about the passion now replace readings about the triumphal entry, which is remembered only in various prayers and suggested hymns. A friend, disturbed by the change, wrote to ask if some fundamental theological issue lay behind this apparent "demotion" of Palm Sunday.

The combination of these two Sundays into one rightly underscores the fact that genuine Christian celebration always has over it the shadow of the Cross. All authentic praise rises from gratitude for

Christ's sacrificial death for our sins. This is, in fact, a distinctively Christian contribution to the idea of praise. In the Old Testament, praise is primarily the creation's uninhibited joy in its Creator (see Ps. 19:1-6; 96:11-13; Hab. 3:3). But in the New Testament, praise is a thankful appreciation for God's supreme and costly gift of Himself (see Rom. 5:2; Phil. 2:6-11; 4:4; Col. 1:12-24; Heb. 12:18-24).

Into the Pit

Why must there be this focus on the death of Jesus? The answer lies in an understanding of the five words in the Apostles' Creed which seek to express what happened at the cross: "He suffered under Pontius Pilate, was crucified, dead, and buried. He descended into hell."

All authentic praise rises from gratitude for Christ's sacrificial death for our sins.

Placed together in the Creed, these words—suffered, crucified, dead, buried, and descended—emphasize first of all how very far God went in identifying with the human condition. But of course this presupposes a belief that Jesus is the only Son of the Father.

Had Jesus been only a teacher or a prophet or a great religious leader, whose teachings were "valid" because they correlated with religious ideas grounded in the general religious awareness of humankind (as so many over the centuries have viewed him),[1] history would have judged His suffering a tragic mistake, on a par, for example, with the death of Socrates. Only if Jesus is fully God does the tragedy of His death really change anything. Herein lies the modern dilemma. Because so many modern people have trouble with Jesus' divinity, they cannot fathom the meaning of His death.

On the other hand, if Jesus had been sent to earth to reveal the glory of God as a purely divine figure, with a human body but not a human nature, His death would have been equally unnecessary. A God who by definition is separate from the realm of matter, could not have really suffered for us.[2]

In confessing in the Creed that Jesus Christ the Son of God was "born," we are saying that everything that happened to Him as a man also happened to God. The two cannot be separated. Once this fact is truly grasped, we can only say these next words in the Creed with stunned amazement: God suffered, was crucified, died, was buried, and descended into hell. What a thought! But why should it have been necessary for God to do all that?

These dark words in the Apostles' Creed speak of the amazing descent of God from His glory into the pit of human misery. They describe a God willing to leave His heavenly throne to endure the grime of political intrigue and nationalistic pride, the strife of religious rivalry, and the hate, alienation, and suffering of life on this planet.

> For certainly no seed ever fell from so fair a tree into so dark and cold a soil as would furnish more than a faint analogy to his huge descent and re-ascension in which God dredged the salt and oozy bottom of creation.[3]

There are, of course, those who find this language of "descent" and "re-ascension" highly objectionable. To regard God as one "up there" who must come down to us is a relic of a primitive, three-storied view of the universe (heaven-earth-hell), with which the Christian faith has been unfortunately associated for centuries. They insist that all talk of descent and return must go.

In the early sixties Bishop John A. T. Robinson's controversial book *Honest to God* argued that the image of a God "up there" had outlived its usefulness to the church. It ought to be jettisoned for a new image of God "in the depths," according to the Freudian imagery that was in its heyday. Drawing on insights from Paul Tillich, who argued that God is to be thought of as the "Ground of Being," Robinson and a whole generation of clergy who followed him called for a revolution in which traditional theism would be replaced by a view of God as the "ground, source, and goal of existence."[4]

Such thinking is far from dead. An Episcopal bishop went on record recently saying that, in the light of this new paradigm shift, it is not credible to believe that God should actually have "sent" His Son to be incarnate of a virgin in order to save humanity from sin. To this leader, who in his ordination as bishop pledged himself to be a "defender of the faith," all such language is a mythological construction of a much deeper truth.

The Human Condition

But has *descent* always been understood in spatial rather than in relational terms? When we speak of someone "coming down to our level," "marrying beneath oneself," "bottoming out," "riding high," or "floating on a cloud," are we speaking spatially? When we say that someone "stoops to conquer," are we not talking more of heartache than of backache? If we do not have to leave the ground to "jump for joy," why must we lock the biblical writers into a literal spatial metaphor, as the modern demythologizers suppose?[5]

The descent of the Creed is a descent from the heights of glory into the depths of the human condition. From the Incarnation to the Crucifixion Christ was God, fully and totally identifying with us. God did not observe suffering; He suffered. God did not learn about torture; He was tortured. God did not have a brush with death; He experienced death. He was buried. Nor did God read about hell; He visited it.[6]

How seriously flawed we understand the human condition to be inevitably colors how we view what God did in dredging the "salt and oozy bottom of creation." Many are tempted here to rush to the twentieth century existentialist writers who, often with great literary skill, describe the human condition in such terms as imprisonment, plague, despair, meaninglessness, and angst. Such insights are valid to a point but ultimately inadequate to do justice to the human condition. For a more profound view we must look to the Bible.

The Abyss

In the book of the prophet Jonah we encounter a man called to the unpopular task of preaching to a corrupt, foreign city. To avoid his mission, he flees from the presence of God. When the sailors who are desperately trying to stabilize their ship in a terrifying storm confront him, Jonah reveals his guilt and accepts responsibility for what is happening. His solution is radical: "Pick me up and throw me into the sea; then the sea will become calm for you. For I know that this great tempest is because of me" (1:12). Reluctantly, the sailors comply. Once in the sea Jonah is swallowed by a great fish, in whose belly he finally realizes his true condition. *In extremis* Jonah turns to the Lord and offers a profound prayer, which forms the substance of chapter 2.

On one level, Jonah is Everyman, for the biblical writer would argue that all have turned away from God's will and sought to do their own. Jonah's condition is the human condition. But what precisely is that condition? Jonah is not simply "lost" and in need of direction and guidance. Nor can his plight be psychologized as merely "depressed," tossed and turned on a sea of emotions, and in need only of a bit of firm ground under his feet. Nor is it adequate to say that Jonah's problem is simple disobedience and the solution repentance—a new resolve to go and preach as God had first demanded.

It has been said that every heresy begins with an inadequate view of sin. Our understanding of Jonah's problem, therefore, is a significant clue to understanding the human condition and crucial to understanding what God had to do to remedy it.

Jonah's problem is far more serious than a lack of direction, or depression, or disobedience. Jonah, in fact, is dead. He is cast out, cut off, and his life is cut short. The imagery of the story must be taken into full account. In the Bible, water frequently symbolizes death. At the beginning of creation the waters cover the void, which is a kind of primeval chaos, an abyss (see Gen. 1:2). For Noah in the Flood (see Gen. 9:15), for Moses in the Red Sea (see Ex. 15:10, 19), and for Joshua at the Jordan (see Josh. 4:18), water is the power of death by drowning. Therefore, when Jonah speaks of being in "the deep," the "floods," the "pit," and at the "moorings of the mountains" (Jonah 2:3, 5, 6), all are symbols of death.[7] No wonder Jonah says "I have been cast out of Your sight" (v. 4) because in the Bible death is accompanied by dereliction. Moreover, the great fish is not, as the children's story books often imply, the symbol of providence, as if Jonah were safe once inside its belly. The fish is the great monster of the deep of whom prophets speak: Leviathan in Isaiah

(27:1), Behemoth in Job (40:15), and the Beast from the Sea in Revelation (13:1). What we are being told is that when Jonah flees from God, as every man and every woman does, the result is death.

The analysis of the human condition in the book of Jonah echoes the analysis found throughout the Bible: apart from God, we are "dead in trespasses" (Eph. 2:1).

In the belly of the monster, in the depths of the sea, cast out from the presence of the Lord and seemingly deserted, Jonah discovers God is there for him in the abyss even in his sin. Once he realizes the mercy of God beside him in the depths, Jonah is freed to take full responsibility for all that has happened, cry out in repentance, and discover the graciousness of God.

Sharing Our Pain

The Creed strongly emphasizes that in Jesus God suffered. To enter fully into the human condition, God had to experience the pain of death and the dereliction of being "apart from Himself." It is true, the Gospels minimize the gory details of the Crucifixion, possibly because its horrors as a means of execution were commonly known in those days. Also it may have seemed important to gospel writers to highlight the non-physical aspects of Jesus' pain. Undoubtedly the rejection, mockery, humiliation (crucified victims hung naked on their crosses, not in the polite loincloths added by later artists), loneliness, and desertion by his friends all caused unimaginable pain. These were the greatest stumbling blocks to Jews accepting Jesus as the Messiah, because physical pain was less of a scandal than humiliation.

Nevertheless, it is too easy nowadays to forget the excruciating physical suffering which Jesus endured. After being scourged with a deadly whip that contained sharp little pieces of metal and bone, an experience which itself left some men either raving mad or dead, the victim would be kicked and dragged to his feet and compelled to carry the timber crossbeam, called a *patibulum*. He would then be driven on by blows from the flat edge of a sword or goaded with its pointed end to his place of execution. The patibulum would then be thrust beneath his neck, his arms gripped and then tied to it with cords, and his hands nailed to it with heavy iron nails that were square in section. The actual nailing would take place either through the palm or the forward fold of the wrist. This was intended to prevent the hands jerking free during the convulsions that crucifixion produced.

The crossbeam would then be hoisted up and attached to the upright beam which was called the *stipes*. It was secured in a special notch prepared for it. Other cords would then tie the victim by the waist to the stipes, and finally the feet would be nailed either with one nail between the metatarsal bones of the two crossed insteps, or with two nails, one through each heel behind the Achilles tendon. There the victim remained hanging until he died, which might be seven, eight, or nine days later. No wonder Pilate was surprised by Jesus' speedy death on Good Friday! Crucifixion was "a death of movement, ceaseless movement, ceaseless writhing and twisting, seeking for some relief, some lesser pain, some temporary stay on death, some lull in the onslaught on the senses, an easement which cannot be found, for there is none."[8]

By confessing our faith in a suffering God we are saying that our God knows what it is like to be a victim. God has taken His place alongside all who, either because of their own faults or the faults of others, experience pain. The fulfillment of Isaiah's prophecy that Messiah would "carry our sorrows" was the Cross (53:4).

Shortly after the end of the First World War, when the memories of that terrible conflict in which there was such enormous loss of life were still fresh in British minds, Edward Shillito illustrated the pain of God's identification with us.

If we have never sought, we seek Thee now;
  Thine eyes burn through the dark, our only stars;
We must have sight of thorn-pricks on Thy brow,
  We must have Thee, O Jesus of the Scars.

The heavens frighten us; they are too calm;
  In all the universe we have no place,
Our wounds are hurting us; where is the balm?
  Lord Jesus, by Thy Scars, we claim Thy grace.

If, when the doors are shut, Thou drawest near,
  Only reveal those hands, that side of Thine;
We know today what wounds are, have no fear,
  Show us Thy Scars, we know the countersign.

—| 93 |—

The other gods were strong; but Thou wast weak;
They rode, but Thou didst stumble to a throne;
But to our wounds only God's wounds can speak,
And not a god has wounds, but Thou alone.[9]

Bearing Our Sins

The language of Scripture forces us to look beyond the physical pain to an even deeper meaning of the Cross. Douglas Webster has written that "at the birth of the Son of God there was brightness at midnight; at the death of the Son of God there was darkness at noon."[10] To explore that darkness we need to see that, in addition to sharing our sorrows and our pain on the cross, Jesus bore our sin. The New Testament unashamedly uses the language of the law court to describe what this means. On the Cross God sided with us against Himself.

Nothing is so evident in our reaction to our own sins as a tendency to self-justification. To avoid the imputation of guilt, we turn our own misdeeds into occasions for blaming God. It doesn't take much to see that it was just such behavior that sent Jesus to the cross in the first place. He "voluntarily accepted liability for our sins;"[11] God in Christ became a "curse" for us, becoming sin itself (Gal. 3:13; 2 Cor. 5:21). His cry of dereliction, "My God, My God, why have You forsaken Me?" signified that the imputation of our sin brought dislocation into His communion with the Father. Thus, as P. T. Forsythe put it, "God honored the law while saving the guilty. He took his own judgment."[12] In this way God emptied sin of its ability to hold us in its grip through the law's power to condemn (see Rom. 6:6). The scriptural evidence for the accuracy of this interpretation is so abundant that all Christians should confess it gratefully.

Angolan Diary

During a recent visit to the People's Republic of Angola, I observed that the church was thriving under communism, despite years of privation, war, suspicion, and isolation. While there I was told of the conversion of an African who had been a drinking, profane, wife-abusing unbeliever. The man's family had suffered much from the unstable volcano within his heart, and many in his village had prayed for him to come to Christ. Then, during an evangelistic meeting, something inside him broke. He responded with repentance and faith; and the heart that had been so filled with hate was now filled with love.

**God emptied sin of its ability
to hold us in its grip.**

This man expected that his sudden transformation would instantly be evident to his wife. In the full flush of his new enthusiasm, he rushed home to tell her the good news. Stony-faced, she heard him tell of God's love, of the forgiveness of sins, of the

Spirit's power to cleanse and renew. Then she took a heavy stick and began to beat him, saying, "You tell me how you like the beatings you've given me." The burly African bent low under her repeated blows, but he refused to retaliate. This went on for days, then weeks. Now that she had found a weakness in her hitherto invulnerable husband, a torrent of verbal abuse locked up within her poured forth. The village prayed. Finally, she realized that the hate within her was no different from the hate that had been in him; and with tears, she too succumbed to the love of her Savior. The great transaction had taken place. Christ had taken her sins. In the end, the cross of Christ claimed another trophy to the glory of God.

Analogies to the Cross can be found in literature, poetry, film, even in nature. It may be helpful to think in medical rather than legal terms. In a feature movie titled *Resurrection,* a woman miraculously receives the gift of healing. After a number of people are dramatically healed through her, a group of doctors decide to test the genuineness of the claims. The woman is brought to a teaching hospital and led into a large operating theater, filled with scientists and doctors. Another woman—twisted and bent from disease—is wheeled in. The camera focuses on the other woman's facial muscles, stretched in a grotesque and painful manner. While the hot lights beam down on the patient, the healer walks up and quietly puts her hand on the woman's stomach. Then she says, "Let me get onto the bed with you." To the surprise of the doctors, the healer climbs up onto the bed and lies by the woman, putting her arm around her in a hug.

At this point, the camera closes in on the sick woman's fingers. They suddenly begin to relax and straighten. Slowly, her entire body unfolds. Tears stream down her face as she is healed.

But then, shockingly, the camera shifts to the hands of the healer. As the hands of the sick woman relax, the fingers of the healer begin to contract. Finally, the sick woman's body is completely straightened, but the healer slides off the bed to the floor, her own limbs now bent and twisted in quivering pain. In a horrifying moment, it becomes clear that the healer has taken the disease into herself in order to make the sick woman whole.

Once we see the Cross as God's way of standing alongside us in our suffering, bearing our sin, assuming our bad will, refusing to be our accuser but instead becoming our accused, we begin to comprehend: for the Bible, for Christian faith, the Cross is the fulcrum, the center of all nature and history. It is, in the poignant phrase of John Stott, the "self substitution of God," God's way of putting Himself into our shoes, that we might step into His.

> *A bee flew near my daughter*
> *A bee buzzed round her head*
> *I moved to protect my daughter*
> *And the bee stung me instead.*
>
> *The pelican was hungry*
> *And hungrier still her brood*

The pelican struck her body
And fed them with her blood.

A brush fire swept the prairie
Consuming everything
A hen was charred concealing
Live chicks beneath her wing.

A judge pronounced a sentence
The guilty could not pay
The judge gave his own money—
And the man went free that day.[13]

The Sign of Jonah

Jesus said, "For as Jonah was three days and three nights in the belly of the great fish, so will the Son of Man be three days and three nights in the heart of the earth" (Matt. 12:40). In other words, Jesus so fully identifies with us that our sin becomes His, our guilt His, our sickness His, and our punishment His. That is why after crying "My God, My God, why have You forsaken Me?" He is still able to say "Father, 'into Your hands I commit My spirit'" (Luke 23:46). The sign of Jonah, which Jesus said would be the only sign given to His generation, is none other than God's willingness to go into the abyss with sinful humanity and there reveal that grace triumphs in the end (see Matt. 12:39; 16:4).

In the Creed, Jesus' descent into hell, whatever else it means, signifies the fact that He fully experienced death for us. There is no realm of human alienation into which God is not prepared to go.[14]

The Good Thief

Across from the famous Kingston Penitentiary on the shores of Lake Ontario, where some of Canada's most notorious criminals are serving time, stands a church with an unusual but entirely appropriate name: The Chapel of the Good Thief.

What made the thief in Luke 23 good? It was hardly his own righteousness, for he frankly admitted his wrongdoing, whereas the other thief crucified with Jesus would not. What made him good was his faith. "Lord, remember me when You come into Your kingdom" (Luke 23:42). In Christ he beheld a man who he knew had committed himself utterly to God's will and was therefore entirely trustworthy. The story of the good thief stands as a challenge to each of us, to put our faith in Christ as he did. Unfortunately, millions make only a sentimental response to the Cross out of pity and sorrow, but that misses the point. Jesus shared our sorrows and bore our sin, so that we might enjoy the benefits of His death and the power of His risen life, through faith.

Once, when I had just finished talking to a group of students at Yale on Paul's letter to the Romans, a charming, self-assured undergraduate approached me with a puzzled look on his face. "I've always assumed," he said, "that our good works and religious activities would be what God looked at in the end, and that he would reward us accordingly." Prayerfully, I did my best to explain that God's standards are so much higher than our own, we are all guilty and in need of grace. The words struck a deep note of response. "If that is so," he said, "I feel completely naked." I was later to learn that this young man was one of the most sexually active students on campus, but he was searching for an alternative to the hedonistic life-style to which he had become addicted. Soon afterward, he found that alternative and is a deeply committed believer today.

Once we understand the depth of our need, we indeed stand naked before God. To define the human condition as "death," as the Bible clearly does, is that necessary blow to our narcissistic pride, which assumes that as human beings we can save ourselves. Far from leaving us in despair, it brings us to life in Christ—if we are willing to walk through the open door.

Questions for Discussion

1. How does Christ's death link His humanity and His divinity?

2. Why is Jonah both Everyman and a type of Christ?

3. Why does every heresy begin with an inadequate view of sin?

4. What place should the physical sufferings of Christ have in one's devotional life?

5. What is the difference between an emotional response to the Cross and a response of faith?

6

Sign of the Chrysalis

The third day he rose again from the dead

As I looked out on the 520 mourners who had squeezed themselves into every possible space in our downtown church, I could see sadness etched on every face. There were weeping teenagers dressed in school uniforms, there to bid good-bye to a much-loved class leader and struggling to cope with their first real exposure to death. There were friends of the girl's parents showing little outward emotion, yet searching for a way to reach out and say, "If she had been ours . . ." There were caring neighbors who had filled the parents' home with food and flowers, making up with activity for what they could not say with words.

Serena Matthews had not been the only victim of an ecology trip that had turned to tragedy. Across

Toronto another service was being held at the same time for one of the other two teenagers who had been drowned in a freak accident of nature, during the first few days of a field trip to Costa Rica. Under careful supervision, the students had been cooling themselves at the foot of a beautiful jungle waterfall, high in the mountainous central area of the country. Suddenly, a cascade of water from a broken natural dam upriver turned the swimming hole from a peaceful paradise into a raging torrent and swept them to their deaths.

Having said good-bye only days before, the three sets of parents were summoned to a faraway country to identify and claim the remains of their children. It was every parent's worst nightmare come true.

I had been with the Matthews family to support them in their grief and to plan a fitting memorial service. Now, as I looked out on the crowd which had gathered in the July heat, I wondered if I could find the right words.

"Serena loved nature," I began, "yet it was the very nature that she loved that took her life." During her nearly nineteen years Serena had cherished a deep, almost symbiotic relationship with nature. Trees, flowers, the forests, living creatures, and earth itself were of great concern to her. I wanted the gathering to realize the glaring paradox that jumped out at me: It was nature, not any human wrongdoing or neglect, that had robbed Serena of life.

"Nature proved not to be benign," I continued. I

reminded them of the great nineteenth century poet Tennyson's observation in a poem written on the occasion of a close friend's death, that nature is "red in tooth and claw." His understanding was a direct slap at the nineteenth century's tendency to romanticize nature.

"So is nature to be loved," I asked, "and then, when its fierce side is revealed, to be hated? One could ask the same question of God. Many do. But God himself loves nature, with a passion far surpassing ours, a passion measured ultimately by the painful offering through which His Son redeemed it."

I knew I was treading on unfamiliar ground for this largely unchurched crowd, but I pressed home my point.

"Because of God's love for the creation, the stuff which He has made, God is not prepared to see it vanish in the despair of death. Since this creation is flawed, it must be re-created. But it will not simply vanish, any more than that part of nature which we know as the human personality will simply vanish.

"God's re-creation of nature began with the resurrection of Christ. This was God's *NO* to death. It is as well the sign that all that is wayward in nature (including *our* human nature), all that is destructive, and despairing, and deadly, will someday be transformed."

By now a deep hush had fallen over the congregation. These people were not being given the usual sentimental pieties expected on such occasions. They were being challenged to think. I continued:

"This hope in the re-creation of nature, as God originally intended, means that it is right for us to love nature now, even though it can turn on us in unpredictable ways. Why did Martin Luther say that if he knew the end of the world was coming tomorrow, he would still plant a tree today? Because that little tree was a sign of his hope in the renewal of nature, by the God who both created it and conquered the death which seeks to spoil it.

"God who made Serena, and the world she loved so deeply, invites us to give Him thanks, that one day this wounded and wounding creation will be made whole."

A Word in Time

Preaching the Resurrection is always difficult in the face of death. But speaking only in vague terms of immortality neither does justice to the biblical faith nor gets to the heart of the pastoral need. People want to know if they will see their loved one again, not whether some impersonal spirit part of them has survived.

The proclamation of the resurrection of Jesus was the backbone of the young church's message to both the Jewish and the Graeco-Roman world. A brief glance at the sermons in the book of Acts, which represent the earliest Christian preaching, reveals many references to the Resurrection (see 2:24ff.; 3:15; 4:33; 5:30; 10:39ff.). The epistles of Paul, which were the earliest New Testament books written, underscore that the Resurrection was "first," that is in importance, to him (1 Cor. 15:3). Subsequently, the need to have a written record of the events of Jesus' life caused Christians to invent a whole new literary genre, gospels, the fundamental assumption of which was the Resurrection, as recognized by virtually all modern scholarship.[1]

Why did the message of the Resurrection spread so rapidly in the first-century world? Michael Green, in *The Empty Cross of Jesus*, cites four ways in which the world was uniquely prepared. First, the idea of vicarious, atoning sacrifice was embedded in both Jewish and pagan literature. For example, it was a common theme in Greek tragedy.[2] Second, the people were longing for a savior. The Jews awaited their Messiah, of course, but even the Romans, who traditionally disliked kings, were tired of a century of civil war, and willing to call an emperor like Augustus "the savior of the world." Third, there was a widespread feeling of guilt, reinforced by a growing consensus that there was one God after all, to whom all peoples were responsible. Last, people felt powerless in the face of death and the general vagueness of contemporary views of the world to come. The popular myth of the phoenix, a bird said to rise from its own ashes to a new life every five centuries, illustrated a pervasive hope for an answer to the problem of death; indeed, it was taken by early Christians as a symbol of Christ's resurrection.

Of course, this analysis does not entirely explain the rapid spread of the message of the Resurrection.

Other writers have noted that traveling evangelism was possible, owing to Roman rule, because "The roads and seas were safe, the pirates and brigands quelled, [and] the frontiers of empire secured."[3] But the overarching factor was that the early disciples were gripped by an unshakable conviction that Jesus had risen. They were willing to put their lives on the line for their belief. By contrast, the old wineskins of Jewish and pagan society were weary of conflict and brimful of questions for which traditional religion had no answers.

Resolving Opposites

None of these factors made the preaching of the Resurrection easy. The idea posed major problems to those locked in traditional Greek and Jewish ways of thought, just as it poses problems for the scientifically minded today, though the problems are somewhat different in nature.

Greek philosophy was unable to reconcile the apparent incompatibility of matter and spirit. The Roman world of the first century, rooted as it was in centuries of Greek philosophical thought, saw no way to bring matter and spirit together. The problem that early Christians confronted was not that people opposed the idea of some kind of union between man and God. In fact, "The union of man with God came regularly through . . . the soul [getting] clear of its body."[4] To the Graeco-Roman mind, death was therefore a release, not a disaster. But educated first-century minds were still not well-disposed to the message of the Christians because one glaring fact stood in the way: Jesus had been raised not only in a spiritual sense, but His *body* had risen to a new and glorious life. The New Testament writers were at pains to underscore the physical nature of Jesus' risen body, in order to guard against a natural Greek tendency to spiritualize the Resurrection (see John 20:27; 21:13–15; 1 Cor. 15:42–49).

Despite this "scandal," or perhaps because of it, the early Christians boldly asserted that God had exalted "the man Jesus" to a place of preeminence in the universe by raising Him from the dead. All "things" had been put under His feet, in Him all "things" consist or hold together, and one day all "things" would be united under His rule, they claimed (see Eph. 1:10, 20–22; Col. 1:17). When asked how such a hitherto unbridgeable gap between the unchangeable world of divinity and the corruptible world of humanity had been bridged, they replied that it was bridged by God's power. The Resurrection was the living demonstration of the "exceeding greatness of His power" (Eph. 1:19).

Jewish minds were troubled by a dualism different from that which plagued the Greeks. For them the apparent irreconcilability was between mercy and justice. Although the Jews believed that God was both merciful and just, they found no way to harmonize these opposites in their experience. Consequently, while they cherished the message of mercy in theory, they cried out for justice and vengeance against their oppressors and the unrighteous, and the immoral in practice (see Ps. 137:8, 9; 139:19–22).

Nothing offended the Jews more deeply than the idea that the Messiah could have been crucified. That God would permit such humiliation could only have meant that God in His justice found Jesus' ministry unacceptable. Jesus was undeniably merciful. His entire ministry had been a demonstration of remarkable compassion, and the people loved Him for it. Nevertheless, how could He have been the Messiah if the manner of His death gave irrefutable proof that God had turned away from Him? Had not God said in Deuteronomy, "He who is hanged [on a tree] is accursed of God" (21:23; see also Gal. 3:13)? Logically speaking, all crucified people are cursed by God; Jesus was crucified; therefore, Jesus was cursed by God.

But in reply Christians said, "Yes, Jesus *was* cursed by God; but because He was God, it was God in Him bearing the curse that rightly belonged to us." He was "delivered up because of our offenses, and was raised because of our justification" (Rom. 4:25). The Christians were in effect saying, God must burst your logical box. God's sovereignty guarantees that He acts in complete freedom. His freedom to act in accordance with His own agenda for salvation, even in the face of the worst that we could do to stop Him, became the core of their proclamation. The gospel was quite simply, "the power of God to salvation" (Rom. 1:16; see also Acts 10:39–43).

The Perennial Challenge

A modern dualism, equivalent in potency to those of the first-century Graeco-Roman and Jewish world views, has been rooted deeply in our secularized minds. Today the issue is the divorce between the so-called real world of everyday events and the spiritual world of religion. To modern minds this divide cannot be bridged. This is why to compel belief today, more is needed than the mere announcement of the Resurrection. Some demonstration of its present power is essential as well.

Although Paul was mocked by the majority of his listeners in Athens, his message was backed up by dramatic healings, notable rescues, gifts of tongues and prophecy, and a growing company of people delivered from immorality, greed, racial and religious prejudice, and hopelessness. These were signs that the new age of the kingdom had already begun and that the Spirit of Jesus had been poured out upon all flesh. No wonder, when the Christians were told to keep quiet, they replied, "We ought to obey God rather than men," and "We cannot but speak the things which we have seen and heard" (Acts 5:29; 4:20).

The Resurrection message will always reveal deep-seated prejudices because of its insistence that we not try to tear asunder the world that God has called one. I recall an experience some years ago when the newly appointed headmaster of a large, nonsectarian boys' boarding school in New England invited me to preach on Easter. I was friendly with the headmaster and had spoken at the school's regular Sunday evening hymn sing prior to his appointment. I assumed that the new headmaster—knowing of my lack of hesitation to speak directly and openly of Christ—had decided that Easter would be an appropriate time to have me. Easter that year fell during term time when students would be in school, so it seemed an ideal match.

In my talk, rather than argue the fact of the Resurrection, I merely drew out some of the implications of the Resurrection for everyday life, on the assumption that Jesus Christ was raised from the dead. I wanted the boys to see that if the Resurrection had really happened, it had life-changing implications.

The beautifully restored, eighteenth-century chapel sparkled that morning as sun streamed through the blown glass windows and flooded the white interior with light. There was none of the shuffling and squirming that usually accompanied "boring talks," and I was sure I had caught the boys' attention. Afterward a group of interested students, including a Jewish boy whom I knew, gathered around to ask questions. I left after lunch, feeling that I had given a good day's work, well worth the three hour's drive into the New England countryside.

Not long afterward, however, I received a call from the headmaster. He thanked me but added that almost as soon as I had left, he had received a delegation of faculty objecting to the content of my sermon and questioning his policy as the new headmaster to show favoritism to one religious group in the school over another. Caught between his own sympathies and those of his secular faculty, he did what any self-preserving employee would do. He told me he could not invite me back.

Easter Every Week

What that faculty may not have realized is that Christians proclaim the resurrection of Jesus Christ, not just on Easter, but every week of the year. Sunday is the day of worship for Christians because on that day Jesus rose from the dead. Otherwise, would not Saturday have remained the day of worship for the new messianic Christians, as it still is for Jews? Sunday by Sunday in churches around the world, Christians recite the Creed that says "on the third day he rose again from the dead." As Christians take Holy Communion they are not remembering a dead Lord but by faith feasting on a living one! At baptism every child or adult is plunged symbolically into the waters of death and raised to a new life in union with Christ. Every Christian burial includes the assuring words that the grave has no final victory. How could that faculty have conceived of a Christian preacher who would not unsettle those unprepared to entertain the idea of the Resurrection?

The early Christians believed unswervingly that Jesus Christ had broken the bonds of death. God had vindicated Jesus' self-sacrifice on the cross. As a result, anyone who believed in Jesus could know, as they did, a pardon from all guilt and an inner cleansing of the conscience that opened the door to a free and loving relationship with God. They claimed that Christ was within to empower them, beside to comfort them, beneath to support them, above to correct them, and ahead calling them to witness that in every area of life He was Lord.

Little Boxes All Made of Ticky-Tacky

The point at which the Resurrection challenges current prejudice is the boxes into which people try to put God. The Resurrection breaks the scientific box that says that anything violating the laws of nature cannot possibly happen. It breaks the secular humanist box that says that this life is all there

The religious leaders of the first century moved swiftly to squash the new movement.

is. It breaks the hedonistic box that says that because this life is all there is, we should "eat, drink, and make out with Mary for tomorrow we die." It breaks the mystic box that insists that, since all life is spiritual, no one life (that of Jesus) was special. It breaks the relativistic box that, while valuing the ethical teaching of the Bible, refuses to accept its claim to be absolute. And it breaks the traditional-

ist box that encases God in stained glass and prevents people from coming to terms with Him
personally.

> *He has burst his three days' prison;*
> *Let the whole wide earth rejoice:*
> *Death is conquered, man is free,*
> *Christ has won the victory.*[5]

The authorities in Jerusalem thought that they
had dispatched Jesus to the grave forever. They had
no time for the sentimental, guilt-ridden Judas who
returned the ransom money in a fit of remorse (see
Matt. 27:3–10). Their goal had been to control the
damage Jesus was causing to their spiritual authority over the people. Their hastily trumped-up story
that the disciples had come and stolen the body was
witness to the deep trouble they knew they were in.
But upon hearing the apostles proclaim the Resurrection, the people were "cut to the heart" (Acts
2:37).

Just as the ancient Jews had tried to silence their
prophets, so the religious leaders of the first century
moved swiftly to squash the new movement. As Jewish writer Abraham J. Heschel said: "To the patriots
[the prophets] seemed pernicious; to the pious multitudes, blasphemous; to the men in authority, sedi-
tious."[6] But the apostles knew that although the
prophets had been mocked, thrown in pits, sent off
into exile, and slain, they had never been forgotten.
They too had shattered the boxes people made for
God.

Efforts to Suppress

History records the irrepressibility of Christians. "What shall I do with these Christians who sing hymns to Christ as to a God?" wrote a confused Pliny the Younger, the local governor, to the Roman Emperor Trajan in the early years of the second century. Pliny had been killing believing men, women, boys, and girls, but now he wondered if he should go on killing them all, or only certain ones? Despite the Christians' exemplary lives, they simply would not bow down and worship the statues of Trajan![7]

===================

The Resurrection survives the efforts of skeptical intellectuals to deny it.

===================

Not only pagans have resisted the message of a God who cannot be boxed in. Resistance has come from within the church as well. Dostoevsky's famous fictional account of the Spanish Inquisition parallels the reality of history. Ivan Karamazov imagines the Cardinal of Seville conveniently placing Jesus in a prison cell and then approaching Him at night with these words:

You suffered for their freedom . . . You wanted man's free love so that he should follow you freely. . . . We have corrected your great work and have based it on miracle, mystery and authority. And men rejoiced that they were once more led like sheep and that the terrible gift which had brought them so much suffering had at last been lifted from their hearts.[8]

To the great Russian novelist, the church had often imprisoned her Lord.

In more modern times, the rector of a fashionable Manhattan church was known for his skepticism about the empty tomb. During his Easter Sunday sermons the assistant clergy used to signal to each other, either thumbs up or thumbs down, depending on whether the rector that year left Jesus in the tomb or got Him out!

Jesus' resurrection survives the efforts of political and ecclesiastical authorities to suppress it. The Resurrection also survives the efforts of skeptical intellectuals to deny it. After the French Revolution many intellectuals tried to invent new religions to replace the supposedly outmoded Catholic church. Robespierre had one idea. Lepeaux had another. Finally, Talleyrand, the Minister of Foreign Affairs, had this to say: "Jesus Christ, in order to found His religion, was crucified and rose again. [Perhaps] you should try something like that?"[9]

Hunted, arrested, imprisoned, and eventually hung on April 9, 1945, by the Gestapo, Dietrich Bonhoeffer, a young German theologian, kept many of his jottings concealed from the police. They eventually were printed in 1953 under the title *Letters and Papers From Prison*. In one he wrote:

We are much more concerned with getting over the act of dying than with being victorious over death.

Socrates mastered the act of dying; Christ overcame death. There is a real difference between the two things. The one is within human capacity, the other implies resurrection. We need the resurrection of Christ to invigorate and cleanse the world today. To live in the light of the resurrection—that is the meaning of Easter.

Bonhoeffer was holding a small service with some of the other prisoners in the prison in Flossenburg when two menacing-looking men in civilian clothes opened the door and said: "Prisoner Bonhoeffer, get ready to come with us." It was a standard command of which all prisoners knew exactly the meaning: death. As the others were bidding him good-bye, he drew one man aside and said, "This is the end; but for me [it is] the beginning of life."[10]

The Empty Tomb: Hoax or History?

The empty tomb was, of course, the claim the gospel writers insist on. However, many today want to affirm the Resurrection as a spiritual truth without committing themselves to this unnecessary, troublesome detail. British theologian G. W. H. Lampe, for example, in a curious twist of logic, argued that "a resurrection of Jesus' physical body, such as is implied by the empty tomb and by some of the stories in the Gospels of his appearances, would point towards a docetic Christ who does not fully share the lot of men."[11] But if physical resurrection denies somehow the finality of human experience, does this not prove the Gospels' point rather tha Lampe's?

Michael Green admits that the empty tomb may not bear the apologetic weight sometimes placed upon it by those who see it as the crowning evidence that Jesus rose, but he does find compelling evidence for its historicity. In a careful study, he argues: First, the four Gospels clearly teach it. Second, naturalistic theories which seek to explain away the disappearance of Jesus' body fail to explain all the reported facts. For instance, why would the Jewish authorities have been so troubled had it been a purely spiritual resurrection? Third, there is the matter of the Roman guard. While dismissed by some as Christian propaganda to counter the claim that Jesus had never really died, the story of the guard is mentioned in two second century Christian writings other than the Gospels, lending weight to its enduring credibility.

Finally, there is the matter of the grave clothes. John mentions that they were in a place by themselves, wrapped up (presumably like a chrysalis). Seeing them was sufficient to cause Peter and John to believe (see John 20:6–8). Had the body been stolen or hastily squirreled away, the grave clothes would either have disappeared with the body or been strewn all over the place. But as Green writes, "he left the grave clothes behind as the butterfly emerging to a new dimension of life leaves the cocoon behind it." As Joseph Klausner, a Jew, writes, unless there was an empty tomb the story doesn't hold water psychologically: "Impossible. Deliberate imposture is not the substance out of which the religion of millions of mankind is created . . . The nineteen hundred years' faith of millions is not founded on deception."[12]

Had the body been stolen or hastily squirreled away, the grave clothes would either have disappeared with the body or been strewn all over the place.

The Creed does not simply say that *a man* rose from the dead. This would place it alongside modern tabloids which abound with stories of this plumber or that hairdresser who "came back from the dead." Christians say that *this man* rose from the dead—this man who was altogether unique from start to finish, in whom even His enemies could find no fault (see John 8:46).

Nor does the Creed say that Jesus simply returned to this life. He was altogether victorious over death. The body with which He returned was not only physical; it was glorious—full of the radiance of God. Jesus was elevated to the place of preeminence in the universe, where He now reigns (see Col. 1:18).

Truth on Fire

Can one truly believe the Resurrection without being energized by its power and set on fire by its truth? Think of the implications. History is not merely the ebb and flow of events in some random or cyclical pattern. Rather, history is purposeful, part of a greater plan, and moving toward a glorious consummation of which the Resurrection is the first sign (see 1 Cor. 15:20–25).

The Resurrection infuses us with a motive for struggling for justice, peace, and truth on earth because it declares that such a struggle is never futile, but rather in harmony with the deepest undercurrents of reality. In God's time right will prevail.

The Resurrection commits us to the fight against everything that controls others through fear of death: sickness, crime, oppression, hunger, greed, and spiritual darkness.

The Resurrection instills a hope that resists despair, fatalism, and the twilight of meaninglessness. "To believe in Christ's rising and death's dying is ... to live with the power and the challenge to rise up now from all our dark graves of suffering love," wrote Nicholas Woltersdorff on the occasion of a son's death from a climbing accident.[13] He and Serena's parents and so many others have found the strength to go on.

Through the Door

In his "Seven Stanzas at Easter," John Updike, the celebrated American novelist, captured the importance to the church of the reality of the Resurrection.

Make no mistake: if He rose at all
It was as His body;
If the cell's dissolution did not reverse,
*   the molecules re-knit,*
*   the amino-acids rekindle,*
The Church will fall.

It was not as the flowers,
Each soft Spring recurrent;
It was not as His Spirit in the mouths and
*   fuddled eyes*
*   of the eleven apostles;*
It was as His flesh: ours.

The same hinged thumbs and toes,
The same valved heart
That pierced—died, withered, paused, and then
*   regathered*
*   out of enduring Might*
New strength to enclose.

Let us not mock God with metaphor,
Analogy, side-stepping transcendence;
Making of the event a parable,
*   a sign painted*
*   in the faded credulity of earlier ages;*
Let us walk through the door.

The stone is rolled back, not papier-maché,
Not a stone in a story;
But the vast rock of materiality that in the slow
*   grinding of time*
*   will eclipse for each of us*
The wide light of day.

And if we will have an angel at the tomb,
Make it a real angel,

Weighty with Max Planck's quanta, vivid with hair
  opaque in the dawn light,
  robed in real linen
Spun on a definite loom.

Let us not seek to make it less monstrous,
For our own convenience,
  our own sense of beauty,
  embarrassed by the miracle,
And crushed by remonstrance.[14]

Questions for Discussion

1. If nature is sometimes hostile to us, why is nature part of God's eternal plan?

2. Why was the Resurrection of first importance to Paul?

3. What stumbling blocks prevent people from believing in the Resurrection today? What boxes do people put God in today?

4. What signs today are evidence of the Resurrection?

5. How crucial to your faith is the story of the empty tomb?

6. Do you think that the Resurrection is connected to the struggle for peace and justice in the world?

7

Humanity on Trial

He shall come to judge the quick and the dead

The family from the West Coast seemed unusually reserved when I first met them in the south of France in 1956. I was an exchange student with the American Field Service program that summer, spending the month with a French family at their summer home, high on a bluff overlooking the blue-green waters of the Mediterranean. The host family had not expected an American mother and her teenage son and daughter to also drop in on their household. However, a general invitation issued over a year earlier had unexpectedly been accepted, and so it was that we all ended up in the same house at the same time. The threesome stayed only a few days, but it was quite clear when they left that something very important had transpired. A sense of peace marked their faces, signaling the resolution of some outstanding problem. As they were very private people, I learned their story only when I discreetly asked my hostess after their departure.

Two years earlier, the father of the family, a senior detective with the FBI, had been brutally murdered. The murderer was on death row in a Nevada prison, awaiting execution at the very time the bereaved family was staying with us. The whole process of apprehending, trying, and convicting the killer had taken a long time, leaving the family emotionally exhausted and deeply scarred. Although they had managed smiles and pleasantries during the visit, their minds were elsewhere and a sadness hung over them like a gray cloud on a winter's day.

In order for choices to have consequences, they must be evaluated and brought before the bar of justice.

But the evening before they left, the mother received a telegram from the U.S. State Department, informing her that the criminal who had murdered her husband had finally been executed. The next morning it was as if a breeze had blown the cloud away. Justice had been done, and they were now free to get on with the rest of their lives.

A Cry for Justice

Some Christians believe that capital punishment is always wrong. They would probably have interpreted the attitude of this family as an unwarranted thirst for vengeance. But it is more plausible that their attitude reflected a simple, innate desire for justice.

In the mid-1950s in England, C. S. Lewis engaged in a protracted argument with the humanitarians of his day over this issue of capital punishment. The humanitarians argued that punishment is only valid if it serves to reform the offender or to act as a deterrent to others. Lewis rejoined that if punishment is permissible only to deter or reform, it severs the vital connecting link between punishment and justice. He maintained that the humanitarians had adopted the metaphor of the hospital. People are sick, and jail will make them well! Justice was not a concern. But Lewis argued that the ultimate question about capital punishment must be, Is it just? Whether punishment deters others is a secondary issue. "It is only as deserved or as undeserved that a sentence can be just or unjust," he said.[1]

Lewis was wrestling with an important issue: the nature of justice itself. He believed that deep within us all there exists a hunger and a longing for justice to be done. If we believe that we live in a moral universe, we assume that choices ultimately matter. But in order for choices to have consequences, there must be a time when all choices are evaluated, a place where they are brought before the bar of justice. In the absence of such a scenario all choices are robbed of meaning.

Arthur Miller, the existentialist playwright, stated the dilemma clearly through Quentin in *After the Fall*:

You know . . . more and more I think that for many years I looked at life like a case at law. It was a series of proofs. When you're young you prove how brave you are, or smart; then, what a good lover; then, a good father; finally, how wise, or powerful or [whatever]. But underlying it all, I see now, there was a presumption. That one moved . . . on an upward path toward some elevation, where . . . God knows what . . . I would be justified, or even condemned. A verdict anyway. I think now that my disaster really began when I looked up one day . . . and the bench was empty. No judge in sight. And all that remained was the endless argument with oneself, this pointless litigation of existence before an empty bench. . . . Which, of course, is another way of saying—despair.[2]

Miller and other existentialists knew that if God were really dead, as Neitzsche had said, then life is meaningless. Humans would still go on asking questions about meaning and purpose, searching for justice and truth, but they would eventually have to admit they were yearning for an illusion.

Jean-Paul Sartre spelled out the implications of this belief. In his study of existentialism, William Barrett writes:

Sartre . . . [noses] out all the sordid and seedy
strands of nothingness that haunt our human
condition like bad breath or body odor. Never in the
thought of the West has the Self been so pervaded
by negation . . . The Self, indeed, is in Sartre's
treatment, as in Buddhism, a bubble, and a bubble
has nothing at its center.[3]

Given that the "endless litigation of existence" is
the insuppressible human cry for justification, the
phrase "He will come again with glory to judge both
the quick and the dead" is a welcome part of the
Apostles' Creed. The words affirm that all history
will end not in the frustration of a cosmic question
mark, but in the satisfaction of a divine verdict in
which justice is done.

Coming, Coming, Gone

In the play *Waiting for Godot,* written by Samuel
Beckett, two tramps, Vladimir and Estragon, stand
near a tree beside the road. They are waiting for
Godot—according to most interpretations of the play,
waiting for God. These two hapless men carry on
an interminable conversation with little coherence
and even less progression. The men are uncomfort-
able and sickly. They contemplate suicide by hanging themselves on the tree, crucifixion-style.

The only action in each of the two acts, aside
from the interminable, mindless conversation, is the
brief appearance of a nobleman, Pozzo, and his
slave, Lucky. They come, say a few words, and then

disappear. Vladimir and Estragon keep on waiting—for Godot. They are unsure whether Godot will really come. They wonder if they have the day right, or his name right, or even what they asked him for. At one point they are told that Godot is not going to come today, but tomorrow. They wait. The next day they are told that it will again be tomorrow. They agree to leave; but they do not. They continue waiting. Finally, the play ends.[4]

Beckett, who had rejected Christian belief but, like other existentialists, found no meaningful alternative, was obsessed with nothingness. It is widely considered that he took the idea for *Waiting for Godot* from Augustine's commentary on the two thieves crucified with Christ. Augustine wrote: "One of the thieves crucified beside Christ went to Heaven. Do not despair. The other thief went to Hell. Do not presume."[5]

Beckett, like Miller, believed that there is in all of us a longing for God to come. Although both playwrights were atheists, they couldn't shake the fundamental assumption that unless God comes, all of us are simply waiting aimlessly for nothing. Hope for the arrival of God is thus basic to human nature. It includes a cry for help, as in Beckett, and a cry for justice, as in Miller.

The Day of the Lord

For centuries the Jews of the old covenant looked forward to what they called the "Day of the Lord."

On that day God would intervene on behalf of His people against their enemies. Judgment would lead to vindication and then salvation. While the nation of Israel would be the primary focus of God's visitation, the entire cosmos would feel the effects. The prospect was heady, and fervent nationalists relished the prospect of God finally meting out punishment to His—and their—enemies.

**Hope for the arrival of God is
basic to human nature.**

But the prophets added a sobering note. The Day of the Lord would be a time of judgment on God's people too! For them it would be not only a day of vindication, but a day of mourning. God would appear as a refining fire to purify His people. The prophets warned the people to prepare for the Day of the Lord with repentance, asking, "Who can endure the day of His coming?" However, the prophetic message was one of hope as well. Following the time of judgment and purification, there would be a new, resplendent Jerusalem; the dead would be raised, and a time of great rejoicing would begin (see Isa. 13:6; 26; 29; 45:22, 23; 54:12; 60:11, 13, 17; Zeph. 3:8; Zech. 8:20–23; Mal. 3:1–5).

In this Jewish apocalyptic thought, Jesus and the apostles found the imagery through which to communicate the distinctive New Testament hope. In an extensive passage in Mark, Jesus says:

Take heed that no one deceives you. For many will
come in My name, saying, "I am He," and will
deceive many. But when you hear of wars and
rumors of wars, do not be troubled; for such things
must happen, but the end is not yet. For nation will
rise against nation, and kingdom against kingdom.
And there will be earthquakes in various places, and
there will be famines and troubles. These are the
beginnings of sorrows.

But in those days, after that tribulation, the sun will
be darkened, and the moon will not give its light; the
stars of heaven will fall, and the powers in the
heavens will be shaken. Then they will see the Son
of Man coming in the clouds with great power and
glory. And then He will send His angels, and gather
together His elect from the four winds, from the
farthest part of earth to the farthest part of heaven
(Mark 13:5-8, 24-27).

Scholars rightly point out that some of these
prophecies must have referred to the great cata-
clysm of A.D. 70, when Jerusalem was conquered
and the temple destroyed. But in these words are
also found the basis for the church's deep and abid-
ing hope in Jesus' return at the end of the age.

Maranatha

In the writing of the apostles the phrases are
found repeatedly: "that day," "the day of Jesus
Christ," the "appearing of our Lord Jesus Christ,"
the "day of redemption," the "blessed hope," the
"coming of the Lord," the "last time," "the end of all

things," and, of course, "the day of the Lord." From the very earliest preaching in the book of Acts to the gospel of John, one of the last books to have been written, the message is clear: Jesus will return to judge, to save, to consummate this age and usher in the next, and above all, to reign.[6]

At this Second Coming Christ will be revealed, no longer as the Suffering Servant who gave His life as a ransom for many, but now in all his splendor as King and Lord. The Greek words used to describe this are *epiphanea,* "appearing," from which comes the word Epiphany, and *parousia,* meaning "presence" or "arrival." In classical Greek they were the words used to hail the arrival of an emperor or king.[7]

Jesus frequently referred to the manner of His coming. It will be like the lightning that blazes across the night sky, like the sun that rises with the dawn, and like a bridegroom coming with joyful expectation to his wedding feast (see Luke 17:24; 1:78 cf. Mal. 4:2; Matt. 25:10). In other words, His coming will be glorious, personal, and visible. In a more sober vein, He said that He will come like a thief in the night, while we are in the midst of our ordinary duties; at a time unknown even to Himself, but known only to the Father. The coming will be sudden and unexpected (see Mark 13:32; 2 Peter 3:10).

The thrust of these gospel passages, when added to the many other references scattered throughout the New Testament, is to make abundantly clear that Jesus will return in justice to judge righteously.

He will separate those who are His from those who are not, just as a shepherd separates sheep from goats. He will reward all who have followed Him in the way of faithfulness and compassion. There will be both joy and anguish. Above all, there will be surprises (see Matt. 25:31–46). No wonder one of the earliest prayers of the infant church was simply *Maranatha*: "O Lord, come!" (1 Cor. 16:22).

Pendulum Swings

To grasp the core of New Testament teaching is relatively simple. However, there are at least three basic approaches to interpreting these and other passages on the end times that have appeared and reappeared throughout the history of the church.

Selective Literalism

The first approach goes hand in hand with a high view of Scripture and can be called *selective literalism*. Therein are found three major views: amillennial, premillennial, and postmillennial. Each of these literal interpretations focuses on the timing of the Millennium, that is, the reign of Christ, which, according to the closing chapters of Revelation, is to last a thousand years.

Amillennialists, following Augustine, see Christ's climactic reign as symbolic of the age of the church during which Christ reigns in and among His people. Postmillennialists, a group that began in the eighteenth century, see the thousand years' reign of Christ as a spiritual revival yet to come from the widespread preaching of the gospel. This will precede Christ's return. To them Christ returns after (or *post*) the Millennium. Premillennialists believe that the thousand years' reign of Christ must follow His return. Of the three, premillennialists can certainly lay claim to the most literal rendering of the passages in question.

All three views agree, despite differences of interpretation, that Jesus will return to judge, that His coming will be cataclysmic, visible, glorious, unexpected, and universal. As His people, we are to wait, to resist fruitless speculation on the timing of His return, to live godly lives, to be rooted in hope, and to be confident that what God began in Christ Jesus, God will complete. Someday every knee shall bow and every tongue confess that Jesus Christ is Lord (Phil. 2:10, 11).

Universal Restorationism

At the opposite end of the theological spectrum from selective literalism stands a second approach, called *universal restorationism* (also called *universalism*). This view appeals more to the liberal wing of the church, but is able to claim precursors as far back as Origen in the second century and Gregory of Nyssa in the fourth.[8] Universalism focuses on the many "all" verses in the New Testament: "*All* [will] come to the unity of the faith" (Eph. 4:13). "In Christ *all* shall be made alive" (1 Cor. 15:22). God's plan is to unite "*all* things in Christ" (Eph. 1:10). Jesus "is the Savior of *all* men" (1 Tim. 4:10). His death is the propitiation "not for ours [sins] only but *also* for the whole world" (1 John 2:2). "God has committed them all to disobedience, that He might have mercy on *all*" (Rom. 11:32). "Now when *all* things are made subject to Him, then the Son Himself will also be subject to Him who put *all* things under Him, that God may *be all in all*" (1 Cor. 15:28). "*All* flesh shall see the salvation of God" (Luke 3:6).

Universalists posit that to believe both in the sovereign love of God and in hell is inconsistent. Some look to a second chance after death. Others, borrowing the Greek idea of the immortality of the soul, believe that after extensive refining discipline all souls return to God. Whatever the approach, universalists feel a deep revulsion at the thought of eternal suffering, and passionately believe that eventually all will be saved. In the words of British theologian G. W. H. Lampe, "The traditional picture of the Day of Doom is of a God who is powerless to save and redeem to the full."[9]

There are problems with the universalist position, even though it is undoubtedly motivated by compassion. It raises the issue of ultimate authority: the Word of God or some elusive concept like "what Christian conscience can now accept"? If our authority truly is the Word, then we must wrestle with the full weight of biblical teaching on hell.

In a lengthy dialogue with liberal English churchman David Edwards, John Stott says that the wide differences in their views stem from divergent understandings of the human condition. To Edwards, as to Lampe, human beings are essentially intelligent, good, and capable of contributing to their own salvation. Stott writes:

> Evangelicals, on the other hand, while strongly affirming the divine image which our humanity bears, have tended to emphasize our human finitude and fallenness and therefore to insist that without revelation we cannot know God and without redemption we cannot reach him.[10]

If our authority truly is the Word, then we must wrestle with the full weight of biblical teaching on hell.

How, then, are we to understand the "all" verses? They must be seen in the light of Jewish exclusivism. For the most part they mean "all without discrimination" rather than "all without exception." They mean none need be excluded rather than none will be excluded. Salvation is not, therefore, just for the Jews. But "whoever calls on the name of the LORD shall be saved" (Joel 2:32). Their universality is in intent, but not in scope. Faced with Jesus and the apostles' clear witness to hell, it is impossible to live under the authority of the New Testament and remain a universalist, however much one longs for all to be saved.[11] For those who have sought refuge from this dilemma by believing in a universal second chance after death, N. T. Wright of Oxford says that universalism tends to reduce the seriousness of sin. "In a century which continues to witness moral evil of frightening proportions and dimensions, a failure to condemn absolutely would be evidence of basic moral blindness."[12]

Symbolic Realism

Steering a middle path between the two extremes of literalism and universalism is a third view, symbolic realism. Hell is a sad reality, but some frightening images should be avoided, such as God dangling human beings over a fire pit.[13] In today's Western culture such images only trivialize hell, as can be seen from depictions of hell in the funny papers. The real meaning of hell is total and final alienation from the presence of God. In hell all that humans truly value, love, delight in, and find meaning in, is removed; those who end up there face the terrible prospect of being banished from the blessings and the presence of God forever.

Behind the view of symbolic realism lies the conviction that the gift of choice that our Creator has bestowed upon us carries an awesome responsibility. A world in which chosen evil is not condemned would be a world in which chosen goodness could not be admired. Christian realism about our fallen human nature also requires us to realize that, short of a fundamental change within us, none of us would choose to spend eternity with God. Therefore, the possibility remains that some would choose to reject the grace of God forever. The most awesome words in the New Testament may be those of Paul, where he says that "God also gave them up" (Rom.

1:24ff.). Although in the original context the apostle's words refer to God's judgments here on earth, they also mean that God does everything possible to persuade His creatures to love and obey Him. But in the end He lifts His restraining hand and lets us choose our own way.

God's justice demands judgment, but we should resist the idea that judgment is God's primary work. Luther wrote that when God judges, it is His strange work, the work of His left hand. God's right hand is to bless. Nothing should cause us to forget that the one who judges is first and foremost the one who saves. Jesus said that He was sent into the world not to condemn us, but that through Him we might have life (John 3:17). In the light of this primary work of God we can understand the promise to Abraham that his descendants would be as the sands of the sea and as the stars of heaven (Gen. 22:17; Hos. 1:10; Rom. 9:27). If God anticipates a great harvest, why should not we?

Are biblical Christians obliged to believe in the eternal torment of the damned? There is considerable dispute here. Those many verses that speak of the "second death," the "lake of fire," and "outer darkness" may signify ultimate annihilation rather than perpetual torment. Some argue that only if that which is thrown into "unquenchable fire" is itself indestructible can it go on forever being tormented. Therefore, since the wicked are not indestructible, they must be consumed. John Stott writes that "the language of destruction and the imagery of fire seem to point to annihilation . . .

ultimately all enmity and resistance to God will be destroyed."[14]

Yet this leaves unanswered the question of why the damned will be "raised" at all, if they are only to be subsequently destroyed. It seems best to rest the issue in the knowledge that God has not left us a detailed blueprint of His eternal plan, only the abundant evidence of His justice and His mercy. The only compassionate Christian response toward the lost must be that of the prophet Jeremiah. He was so troubled and sorrowful over the waywardness of Israel and the coming judgment that he has been called "the weeping prophet."

Uncomfortable Comfortable Words

The Heidelberg Catechism of 1562 is said to have combined the intimacy of Martin Luther with the charity of Philipp Melanchthon and the fire of John Calvin. It asks:

Question 52: What comfort is it to you that Christ shall come again to judge the living and the dead?

Answer: That in all afflictions and persecution, with uplifted head, I may wait for the Judge from heaven, who has already offered himself to the judgement of God for me, and has taken away from me all curse.[15]

Christians have seen the return of Christ as judge to be a comforting reality. It is but the logical conclusion of all that Jesus began, the consummation of His work on earth. Leon Morris wrote that

Christ's was "a divine love . . . not a careless sentimentality indifferent to the moral integrity of the loved ones. . . . [His is] a love which is a purifying fire, blazing against everything that hinders the loved ones from being the very best they can be."[16] Christ's return in glory to judge is an encouraging reminder of three facts.

God Is Just

It would be impossible for God to overlook the seriousness of sin and still be true to His own nature. We must always guard against compromising the justice of God. To their credit, the most literal interpretations of the Bible's view of the end times seek to honor the just side of God's nature.

God Is Merciful

The same God who accuses us has submitted Himself to our accusation. In His love for humankind God allowed Himself to be put on trial, to be sentenced and tortured to death for our sin, thus saving us by the sacrifice of Himself. God is "not willing that any should perish." It is to the credit of universalism that, despite its fundamental error, it seeks to preserve the wideness of God's mercy.

God Is Personal

To God our lives have a "finite conclusion" but an "infinite importance."[17] God's judgment of us is a measure of our significance to Him and of our importance in creation. It is a mark of our true humanity that we will be held accountable by God for the way we responded both to His invitation to obedient faith in His Son and also to His call to compassionate caring for others (see Matt. 25:31–46, cf. John 3:36).

Packed Bags

The much-loved Pope John XXIII coined a phrase when his health was failing and the public knew that he was dying: "My bags are packed." Picked up by the press, it appeared in newspapers around the world.

His phrase reminds me of the careful preparation that my wife, Sandra, and I made for the birth of our first child. We had been told that the midnight "munchies" frequently draw fathers away from their expectant wives during those critical early morning hours when so many babies are born. We therefore packed a substantial picnic and kept it stored in the refrigerator, in case sudden contractions forced us to rush to the hospital in the middle of the night. A little like the wise young women with oil in their lamps awaiting the arrival of the bridegroom, we were "packed and ready."

Similarly, God tells us to have our bags packed, not primarily in preparation for our own deaths, though that is part of it. Rather, we are to have our bags packed in expectation of the arrival of God's new world, which, like the firstfruits of human love, is groaning and struggling to be born (see Rom. 8:21, 22).

Questions for Discussion

1. Why did Arthur Miller's character need to go on with his "pointless litigation of existence before an empty bench"? How do you relate human significance and God's judgment of us?

2. Why did the early church pray, *Maranatha*?

3. Which of the three ways of interpreting the biblical passages about the end times do you favor?

4. Why is the coming judgment a comfort, and how can we be sure that we will pass the test?

5. What does it mean "to have one's bags packed"?

Go-Between God

I believe in the Holy Ghost

When I opened the front door to let Bill in, I would have known he was back on a marijuana binge, even if a roommate hadn't already told me. Although tanned and healthy after a spring break trip to Key West with college friends, his slovenly appearance was appalling, and his face showed none of its usual fun-loving sparkle. Instead, the guilty look indicated that he hadn't wanted to come at all. Considering the reason we were meeting, I couldn't say I blamed him.

An athletic twenty-year-old, Bill was the second son of a prosperous government lawyer and a cool Irish mother with a biting, sarcastic tongue. Knowing he could match neither his older brother's academic accomplishments nor his two sisters' social ease, Bill threw himself into the macho world of sports, recreational drugs, and one-night stands. He had been kicked out of boarding school for possession of drugs but managed to finish public high school in Washington, D.C.'s fashionable northwest quadrant.

Beneath Bill's surface bravado lay a searching heart and a willingness to commit himself to truth, which led him to commit his life to Christ. But the old demons that had been allowed free rein for several years were not about to give up without a fight. During the three summers he worked on staff of the FOCUS Study Center on Martha's Vineyard, where I was the director and he was the property manager, I became Bill's mentor and friend.

Bill was attempting to be honest about his ongoing struggles to live a consistent Christian life during the times he was not living at the Study Center. His efforts had brought us together as prayer partners, and that contact spilled over into the school year. We stayed in touch through letters, phone calls, and get-togethers during vacations when traveling plans permitted. Bill's bold efforts to walk the straight and narrow were interspersed with major "falls," especially during rugby season when he was surrounded by hedonistic teammates. In addition, like many drug users who show signs of chemical dependency, Bill had a problem with deception.

I made several unsuccessful attempts to confront Bill about his drug problem, including a tension-filled intervention that included a roommate who shared my concern. Finally, I resorted to a written covenant. Bill and I agreed in writing that if he ever lied to me again, he could no longer be a leader in the FOCUS ministry. I knew his involvement meant a great deal to him, as it did to me. We were painfully aware of the consequences if our agreement were broken.

It was nine months later, then, that Bill appeared, disheveled, at my door. We talked for forty-five minutes that afternoon. Our time together ended with a rereading of the covenant and a very sad parting. After he left, I struggled with the thought of having cut him off from his one meaningful Christian connection. But consistency was something Bill needed badly, even if it had a high price tag.

The Helper

Remarkably, this wrenching professional separation did not end our personal friendship. Bill knew that I cared deeply, so we remained in touch even though we were no longer meeting as fellow members of the FOCUS staff. Over the succeeding years, when we could, we hiked, sailed, played tennis, or just talked. Our times were always challenging, and usually included prayer.

Gradually things turned around for Bill. He brought his drug use under some measure of control. He became active in another ministry, joined a local church, and launched a successful business. Today, some seventeen years later, he is a self-styled couch potato with a wife, two children, a station wagon, and a dog, and a faith which, despite its ups and downs, has continued to grow. Bill recently became an elder in his church, chair of its evangelism committee, and leader of a men's Bible study group. He takes an active interest in discipling younger men who are remarkably like the person he once was.

The day I sat down in my study to write this chapter on the Holy Spirit, I hit a mental block. My notepad was filled with scribbled comments, but there was no coherent order or theme to them. On the floor around me were a dozen books on the Holy Spirit which I had either read or skimmed. Time was ticking on, but nothing seemed to flow. Frustration was setting in.

I knew that the Holy Spirit is the "helper," the "Paraclete" as Jesus called him, the One who comes alongside us to enable us to know the Lord and to do His will. So I put down my pen and prayed for help. "O Holy Spirit, be my helper. Help me to know what to say to those who will read what I am writing." It was a short, simple prayer, after which I went back to my notes.

Within minutes the phone rang. I answered it, and on the other end was a voice from the past—Bill, calling from his office, saying that he had just felt like giving me a ring. No, there was nothing special on his mind. All he wanted to say was "thanks." Thanks for all the years of hanging in, for believing in what God was doing in his life, and for listening and caring. In ten minutes the call was over.

I put down the phone and asked myself, "Was

that a coincidence or a God-incidence?" Did it just "happen" that that phone call came when I needed it, or was God answering my prayer for help in a most unexpected way, teaching me something about His mysterious and wonderful Holy Spirit?

We repeat, "I believe in the Holy Spirit" in the Apostles' Creed. But what are we saying? Are we just mouthing an ancient doctrine or are we confessing our faith in the Spirit Jesus said He would send to be our Paraclete, our helper, our Comforter, and our empowerer?

The Eternal Triangle

One evening as I was leading a Bible study in our parish house, I found myself trying to explain the difference between the Christian and Muslim views of oneness to two young Somali men who had joined us.

"How is it that you Christians say that God is One, and yet you believe in the Father, the Son, and the Holy Spirit?" they asked me. "Aren't you believing in three gods?"[1]

The Christian confession of the Holy Spirit as equally God alongside the Father and the Son in the Trinity affirms that God has made Himself known to us as three persons. It also makes a statement about our understanding of unity. If from all eternity there was love, as Christians say, then there had to be both lover and loved, for love needs an object. If from all eternity (before creation itself) there was one who wills, there also had to be one who responds. If from all eternity there was humility, there also had to be one who guides and one who yields. Where do these qualities, which we so admire in human beings, originate? Surely they are not mere animal drives, traceable to some beastly origin. But if they are traceable to God, then they must in some way be rooted within his character. If there is one God, then these qualities imply plurality within that unity.

Without the Trinity, we lose the ability to understand how humanity achieves both unity and diversity. In 1985 Robert Bellah, in a lucid overview of American culture, maintained that "individualism may have grown cancerous . . . it may be threatening the survival of freedom itself." He pleaded for a balance in which our unbridled pursuit of individualism (mythically preserved in cowboys, detectives, and self-made men) would be linked to the renewal of commitment and community.[2]

Five years later, sociologist Reginald Bibby said much the same thing of Canada: Canadian society is consumed with the supreme importance of the individual coupled with a conviction that all is relative.[3] These prophets of communalism are protesting against a culture that produces people who don't need people. In the United States, Bellah says that the survival of freedom is at stake, while in Canada Bibby claims that multiculturalism, which was supposed to ensure the nation's survival, has gone mad. How is the Trinity, and specifically the Holy Spirit, relevant to this problem?

Babel Reversed

On the day of Pentecost, the Holy Spirit, whom Jesus promised to send, was poured out on the eleven disciples who were meeting for prayer early in the morning. The crowd that witnessed the event could not have been a more diverse and cosmopolitan group. All the rival parties that had jockeyed for political and religious power within Israel's national life were, of course, present in Jerusalem. In addition, many pilgrims from all over the Roman world had arrived for the festivities. These visitors, comprising a mosaic of cultural backgrounds, filled the city's streets with a babel of languages and dialects. They were members of the Jewish diaspora who had returned to reestablish a relationship with their roots, as well as a number of Gentile proselytes to Judaism (see Acts 2:5–11).

Around nine o'clock in the morning, a commotion drew the crowd milling around the temple to a group of men who were making a racket. At first, to the confused crowd, the sound was nothing but gibberish; men were all speaking at once, but in different languages. As people strained to listen, however, they began to detect words of praise and prophecy in their own native dialects. Some people, schooled in the Scriptures, would have wondered whether they were experiencing the long hoped-for reversal of the scene at Babel, when at the dawn of history God had judged humanity for its pride by causing a division of culture and languages (see Gen. 11:1–9).

From the day of Pentecost onward, the divided community in Jerusalem began to witness a wholly new phenomenon taking shape. The church was a united, loving fellowship, transnational, transcultural, and trans-linguistic in character, in which the barriers that had hitherto divided Jew from Jew and Jew from Gentile were being broken down. Without sacrificing diversity, the Spirit was creating a new, unifying force of men and women, slaves and free, rich and poor, that set its sights on the conversion of the world.[4] To the apostolic writers, a whole new age had begun, a new humanity had been created, and the perennial problem of achieving diversity within unity had at last been solved (see John 10:16; 1 Cor. 12:12–26; Gal. 6:15; Eph. 2:11–22; Col. 3:15).

Koinonia

It is easy to underestimate the revolution in thought that the apostles' teaching embodied. In cultures where everything depended on one's lineage, religion was expected to reflect the cultural divisions of family, clan, tribe, and nation. Even the Jewish religion was a religion "for men only" in a way that the Christian religion was not. It was also "about Jews only." But according to the apostles' teaching, the Spirit was enabling people with different ethnic, cultural, and racial backgrounds, different gifts, different talents, and even different views on nonessentials, to be one. Their common faith, hope, and love was the telltale sign.

The Spirit's work of uniting diverse peoples continues. Nearly every week, except during the summer, twenty to twenty-five groups of lay people gather across Metro Toronto for Bible study, sharing, and prayer. These small groups have been a vital part of the life of the parish I serve for nearly two decades. No attempt is made to "match" the members of these groups. Singles, married couples, younger and older members mix across the economic, social, and racial spectrum, united by the common goal of maturing together in Christ. Special groups aim to introduce hesitant new members to the idea, most of whom eventually go on to join existing groups or to form new ones. Our word for these weekly gatherings is K-Groups, from the Greek word *koinonia,* meaning "fellowship."

The Spirit unites diverse peoples.

William Barclay tells us that the Greeks used the word *koinonia* in three ways: to describe a business partnership, a marriage, and an individual's relationship with God.[5] The New Testament writers then took this word, with all of its rich association with intimate personal relationships, to use as a synonym for Christian fellowship. To be linked one with another in *koinonia* was to be members of a common family. *Koinonia* meant more than friendship, affinity, association, or membership. This was a common participation in God. Paul uses the word when he speaks of Holy Communion: "The cup of blessing which we bless, is it not the communion of the blood of Christ?" (1 Cor. 10:16).

The Unbreakable Link

In the gospel of John we read that the Spirit's job is to take the things of Christ and make them real to us: the love of Christ that accepts us all on the same basis, unconditionally; the truth of Christ that guides our behavior and gives us a common perspective on life; the joy of Christ that gives us hope in the world to come; and the presence of Christ to correct, guide, help us pray, and empower us to witness for Him (15:26, 27; 16:8–11, 13–15, 24; cf. Rom. 8:26).

For this reason, I believe that we should be wary of the persistent tendency in much current religious thought to identify the Spirit of God with things other than Christ.[6] Some would like to identify the Spirit with art, for instance. The Spirit of God in the Old Testament inspired Bezalel to devise artistic designs for the temple (see Ex. 31:1–5). But is it right to say that we can know the Spirit today through appreciation of art? What about music? Can we say that because the Spirit came upon King Saul whenever David played his lyre and sang (see 1 Sam. 16:23), the Spirit can be known through all music? What about wisdom? In the Old Testament Book of Proverbs, wisdom functioned very much like the Spirit: giving guidance, correction, insight, and leading the believer into truth (1:20–23). But can it be said that wisdom or intelligence are paths for the Spirit to make Himself known today? What about creativity? The Spirit brooded over the chaos in creation and brought order into being (see Gen. 1:2). But are we at liberty to identify the Spirit of God with creation and therefore with creativity generally, as some would propose? What about freedom? Saul was consumed with a kind of prophetic ecstasy. David danced with abandon before the Lord. The wind or breath of the Lord enabled Israel to enjoy freedom from bondage (see 1 Sam. 10:10ff.; 2 Sam. 6:16; Ex. 14:21; 15:8, 10). But can we identify the Spirit today with all political forces and cultural movements that purport to bring freedom and liberation?

We should be wary of the persistent tendency to identify the Spirit of God with things other than Christ.

Unquestionably, the Holy Spirit makes all the blessings of God real to us. No sphere of life is incapable of being animated by His presence (see John 1:9). He is, in John V. Taylor's phrase, the "go-between God," bringing God and His world in touch with each other. But the New Testament makes it clear that the Spirit only goes by way of Jesus Christ.

In the Bible we read that Jesus is the Lord of the Spirit. Jesus promises the Spirit, sends the Spirit, is present by the Spirit, and dwells within us by the Spirit. To be united with Jesus is to be united with His Spirit. Only with the Spirit's help can we truly confess that "Jesus is Lord." The Spirit in the New Testament is the Spirit of Jesus (see John 15:26; Acts 2:33; 1 Cor. 6:17; 12:3; 2 Cor. 3:17). James Dunn puts it simply: "The cosmic power of God, the mysterious and miracle-working action of God in His world, can now be known simply as the Spirit which inspired Jesus and which came from Jesus."[7] And as William Temple has said:

> The Holy Spirit is not merely the diffused power of God discoverable everywhere in the universe; but is first and foremost the special and distinctive influence which God exerts over our souls as we respond to His love in the human life of Christ. . . . After we have begun with Jesus Christ, as the Source of that Spirit, we can afterwards trace his operation over the whole field of nature and history.[8]

Thus, the temptation must be resisted to identify as the workings of the Spirit all those things deemed "good" on other grounds. The work of the Spirit is always to lead us to Christ, and through Him, to the world.

To picture this dynamic clearly, imagine an hourglass. At the top of the hourglass is the broad area into which God pours His Word, His wisdom, His people, and His Spirit. Down through the ages they come. His word is heard through a prophet here, a lawgiver there. His wisdom comes forth from seer and sage. His people are gathered together into one from an assortment of tribes. They multiply and spread. His Spirit alights on a prophet here, a king there, a judge in one place and a shepherd in another.[9] As the sands of time sink, the glass narrows. Down they come until the opening becomes so narrow that only one man stands in the breach. Jesus has become the Word and the wisdom of God. Only those who receive Him receive that Word and wisdom. He chooses twelve disciples as the heads of the twelve new "tribes" of the new Israel. Only those who believe in Him are part of the new Israel. On Him is the Spirit, anointing, empowering, revealing, and passing through Him to all who by faith come to Him. As those who do trust Him go forth, the hourglass widens again. They are given gifts of the Spirit through which to glorify God. They are given eyes with which to see Him at work. They receive a new confidence that in Christ Jesus all things hold together and a solid new hope that one day all things will come under His rule.

Baptized into One Body

The Holy Spirit links us not only to Christ, and through Christ to the world, but He also baptizes us into the body of Christ. Baptism has two dimensions, physical and spiritual. There is, of course, the outward rite of baptism in water by which we become a visible member of the church. But Paul taught that we are also to be baptized in the Spirit inwardly. As the Bible clearly states, it is quite possible to have the outward baptism of water without the inward baptism of the Spirit (see Acts 8:21). It is also theoretically possible to have the inward baptism of the Spirit without having been baptized in water. However, the two were meant to go together as the means whereby we are incorporated into the fellowship of believers.[10]

Every Christian who trusts Christ as Savior and Lord and who loves the "brethren" may be confident of being baptized in the Spirit of Jesus Christ into the body of Christ. To be able to say "Jesus is Lord," to call God "Father," and to love the Christian community are the three indelible signs given in Scripture of having encountered the power and presence of the Holy Spirit (see Rom. 8:16; 1 Cor. 12:3, 13; 1 John 4:12).

To Each His Own

Unfortunately, many distance themselves from the intimacy of Christian fellowship. They stay on the edges of the body of Christ for fear that a closer association will cause them to lose their independence or become carbon copies of other Christians. But Paul teaches specifically to respect diversity. "Are *all* apostles? Are *all* prophets? Are *all* teachers? Are *all* workers of miracles? Do *all* have gifts of healing? Do *all* speak with tongues? Do *all* interpret?" (1 Cor. 12:29–30; italics mine). Only one ingredient binds us—love (see 1 Cor. 13).

The gifts of the Spirit we are given will likely reflect each person's unique blend of talents, characteristics, and personality. Helmut Thielicke says that the Spirit will not likely create something in us out of nothing, but rather will refashion and renew something that is already there: "If each [is given] his own gifts . . . we may indeed assume that in this regard [our] natural presuppositions and gifts [won't be] left out of account." But he warns against thinking that these gifts are simply latent abilities that operate on their own inherent dynamic.[11]

God the Father is sovereign, and the Spirit does His bidding. When the Spirit is allowed to work in freedom, remarkable things happen within the Christian community. We must not be shocked at the great diversity of ways in which the Spirit works: dramatically, emotionally, quietly, gradually, thoughtfully. Just as there are sudden conversions and gradual conversions, Christians receive new gifts on the spot when they need them or see them develop over time. Among the Spirit's many manifestations are a new freedom to care for one another and to tap into extraordinary powers of listening, to praise God in an unknown tongue, and to heal. If we assault those powers of secularism, unbelief, and disobedience that linger in us, we will find ourselves in spiritual conflict with the demonic powers in a variety of subtle forms. Michael Green says that "we should not be embarrassed by the miraculous. When it comes to the Spirit, on the whole people get what they expect."[12]

Personal Renewal

"Revive thy church, beginning with me" is an old prayer that points to the Spirit's renewing work in the believer. In April of 1991 *Reader's Digest* carried a story about the new Archbishop of Canterbury, George Carey. One detail was of particular interest to my congregation at Little Trinity. Many years ago when Carey was a young, relatively unknown clergyman on a visit to Canada, he was invited to preach at our church at a Sunday evening service. In the article Carey admits that his faith had grown a bit stale and his heart was cool. But he managed a sermon that evening and was invited to have a meal afterward. He also stayed for a small group meeting in a dilapidated house adjacent to the church, where some of the students who had attended the service were living in community.

The Spirit moves us from hoping only for ourselves to hoping for all others.

During a time of quiet prayer in the warmth and vitality of that fellowship, George Carey experienced an infilling of the Holy Spirit that renewed his life in Christ. At the time, no one there could have dreamed that the young clergyman who was touched by God's Spirit in such humble surroundings would one day hold the highest office in the Anglican church worldwide. With the Spirit's presence, every church can be a place where extraordinary things happen.

The Holy Spirit always begins His work in the individual, although He always leads to community. He comes when Christ breathes on us and gives new life. As Karl Barth wrote: "When the Spirit approaches me and takes possession of me, the result will be that I hear, am thankful and responsible and finally may hope for myself and for all others; in other words, that I may live in a Christian way."[13]

The Spirit moves us from hoping only for ourselves to hoping for all others. In the words of Emil Brunner, "The church exists by mission as fire exists by burning." Since the chief quality of fire is power to set something else afire, it should not be surprising that when the disciples were filled with the Holy Spirit, they were given a new boldness to speak to others about Christ (see Acts 4:20, 31). As a very reserved businessman recounted his experience of the Spirit: "When I opened my life to the Holy Spirit, I received the gift of tongues—the *English* tongue! You see, I have always been terribly shy, and even had a stutter that kept me from trying to communicate. Then when I had a deeper experience of the Holy Spirit, I found that I could talk to people without fear. I could actually witness to Christ with confidence."

Much ink has been spilled on the controversial subject of speaking in tongues, but rather than attempt a theological analysis of this gift of the Holy Spirit, I close this chapter with my own story.

Christmas Eve

Many years ago, there was a surge in curiosity about the gifts of the Spirit. Many hungered to have a greater sense of the reality of their faith, and soon several friends in the youth ministry where I was involved began testifying to a new, great blessing that they had received in their lives. A new prayer language had been given them directly by the Spirit. From their study of the Bible, they were sure that every Christian should seek this anointing and speak in tongues.

I had my own legitimate theological questions, but more than anything I felt inadequate, especially when I compared my quiet, steady faith to others' overflowing exuberance. I began to feel as if I had nothing to offer unless I experienced what they had. Yet if this anointing was the answer to all one's spiritual ills, why wasn't it taught more clearly in the Bible?

Confused and upset, I decided to take a retreat to a German Protestant convent in New Jersey. During those four days just before Christmas I prayed, walked in the woods, searched my heart, and asked for whatever God had for me. The table in my room was piled high with books arguing all sides of the question.

I had no problem believing that the gift of tongues (*glossolalia*) was a valid manifestation of the Holy Spirit, and therefore did not agree with those authors who claimed the experience was limited to the apostolic age.[14] But I balked at the idea that tongues were the primary evidence of a second experience of grace that all Christians are supposed to have, which some call "baptism in the Holy Spirit." The breakthrough in my understanding came while reading Second Corinthians. Paul had been under similar pressure from a group in Corinth who claimed that tongues and other manifestations of the Spirit were signs of power. Paul rejected the notion that gifts and power were corollaries and insisted instead on a quiet confidence that, through his weakness, the power of Christ would shine. Once I understood those last chapters of the book, I was reduced to tears of gratitude: I was okay. The Spirit could use me just as I was.[15]

But during that time, even as I was wrestling and praying and thinking, I was also seeking to be open. Perhaps God rewarded that in the end. On Christmas Eve, alone in a small church for midnight Communion, something memorable happened. I sensed the presence and power of the Holy Spirit upon me as never before. I didn't speak—I never have spoken—in tongues, but I was touched and anointed that night in an unforgettable way.

Was that a second blessing? Perhaps—or a third or a fourth. On reflection, I suspect that the experience was God's humorous way of saying, "Peter, you were right to conclude that the Bible doesn't teach second blessings, but here's one anyway."

Over the years I've realized that without the Holy Spirit actively filling my life that night and at other times, my life would have been very different. I might have long since given up active evangelism and become a traditional churchman. I probably would have come to accept various blemishes in my character as "the real me," and quietly stopped trying to conform my life to God's Word. Undoubtedly, I would have "moved beyond" simple faith in the Cross for the forgiveness of my sins and begun to follow trendy theological fads. I would have lost my hunger for God's Word and developed a preaching style that was topical, trendy—and above all, brief. I might, in fact, have never bothered to write this book.

Questions for Discussion

1. Is the Holy Spirit the Comforter or the "Discomforter"?

2. Can we legitimately trace human qualities such as the capacity for love back to the nature of God as Creator?

3. What has been your experience of *koinonia*?

4. Why is submission to the lordship of Jesus Christ essential to discovering your spiritual gift(s)?

5. Discuss the connection, or lack thereof, between spiritual gifts and natural talents.

6. How does the Spirit relate to our weaknesses? to our strengths?

Defying the Gates
of Hell

The holy catholic Church,
the communion of saints

After signing the guest book of my gracious host who spoke with a German accent, I began flipping through the pages to see if I might recognize any of his previous guests. It was a thick book and went back several years. Suddenly my eye caught a name that caused my heart to skip a beat: Adolf Hitler.

Naturally, I asked if this was *the* Adolf Hitler and if so, how he had come to be a guest in my host's home. He explained that in Germany prior to World War II, many Christians like himself had pinned their hopes on Hitler to lead Germany out of the doldrums that followed the German defeat in World War I. Many church leaders even publicly supported Hitler's efforts to find spiritual meaning in Aryanism.

The German church's capitulation to Nazism, I later learned, was one of the sorriest episodes in twentieth century Christianity. Until Karl Barth wrote the Barmen Confession in 1933, the document that created the so-called "Confessing Church," many believers supported Hitler. Conservatives, like my host, were taken in by Hitler's economic reforms. Liberals, who espoused a philosophical idealism cut off from the Word of God, had lost the ability to distinguish truth from error.

In deference to anti-Semitic propaganda, churches excised all references to Jewish customs and culture from their liturgies. Hebraisms like *alleluia* and *amen* were dropped out of prayer books and hymnals. In 1936 a well-known bishop produced a revised edition of the Sermon on the Mount. "Blessed are those who mourn, for they shall be comforted" for instance, was changed to the more stoical: "Happy is he who bears his suffering like a man; he will find his strength never to despair without courage." Ernst Bergman, a pro-Nazi theologian, said: "The German God is the Friendly God, not the Jewish tyrant God. I believe in the German God who is at work in nature and the lofty human spirit and in the strength of his people. I believe in the helper Christ, who is struggling for the noble soul."[1]

What on earth had happened to the German church? Had the church simply ceased to be? Had it so conformed to the culture that, at least in official expression, there was merely a reflection of the culture, no longer the "holy, catholic Church, the communion of saints" of the Apostles' Creed?

Christ and Culture

In the Creed we say that we believe in the Holy Spirit, and then, flowing from the Spirit, the "holy catholic Church, the communion of saints." Each of these words is vital and sends us back to the Bible. The church is *holy* because it belongs to Christ and is therefore different from all who do not own allegiance to Him (see 1 Peter 2:9; 1 John 4:4). The church is *catholic* because it is universal, including "all who in every place call on the name of Jesus Christ our Lord" (1 Cor. 1:2). It is also *one,* as stated in the Nicene Creed, regardless of apparent divisions. This does not mean unity under a single administration but unity by one Spirit and one Lord, with only one means of entry, baptism (see John 17:10; Eph. 2:16–20; 4:4, 5).

The Greek word for *church, ecclesia,* means "called together," to signify the response to Jesus' summons to be "called together" as an assembly of God's people.[2] *Communion* indicates partaking of one common life, the life of the Spirit of Jesus Christ, with members therefore belonging to one another (see John 17:26; 1 Cor. 10:15–17; 12:12, 13, 27). It is a communion of *saints* because in the New Testament all who believe in Christ are called saints; not because of their personal sanctity but because having been chosen by Him, they are holy in the sense of being set apart for God (see John 15:16; 1 Cor. 1:2;

Col. 1:2).[3] The church, then, is part of the work of the Holy Spirit.

But how do we reconcile this lofty, biblical view of the church to the disparity we see in churches today? Some have taken refuge in the concept of an "invisible church," that band of real believers within every group that calls itself a church. The rest are only nominal Christians, for all intents and purposes not genuine Christians at all. There are obvious attractions to this view because it is a fact that in many ailing churches a small band of genuine Christian believers forms the core. However, in the New Testament, the church is not invisible. The only church the Bible knows is a visible one.[4]

At the same time, on earth there does not exist the "perfect church." Unfortunately, there are sincere believers who cheerily de-Christianize all religious bodies but their own. They claim that their own is perfect in structure (or doctrine or zeal), and thereby reduce the church of God to their one small sect. They are like the founder of Rhode Island, Roger Williams, who supposedly at one point decided that the true church consisted only of himself and his wife . . . and there were times when he even wondered about her!

H. Richard Niebuhr, in his classic study *Christ And Culture,* argued that the problem grows out of conflicting understandings of how Christ relates to culture. Once that question is answered, the model can be discovered to relate what Scripture says about the church to what we find on earth. Niebuhr identified five basic models of Christ and culture.

Christ Against Culture

A church or denomination that adopts this stance may actively denounce a weakening political tyranny, thus helping to bring about its downfall. This has happened recently in Eastern Europe and Latin America.

**Unfortunately, some sincere believers
reduce the church of God to
their one small sect.**

Christ a Part of Culture

The church may be providing most of the social, educational, and welfare institutions of a country, and the culture and customs of Christianity may be incorporated as those of the country. The Canadian province of Quebec before the Quiet Revolution was an example of this.

Christ Above Culture

This relationship is best expressed through the phrase that Christians are to be "in" but not "of" the world. A manner of accommodation is worked out between the radical demands of Christ and the practical demands of living in the world so that people can live two parallel lives: a religious life and a secular one. Christ's lordship over the secular life is admitted, but not pressed too far. Much of the traditional Protestant church in North America reflects this relationship.

Christ in Tension with Culture

Taking sin more seriously than the church which puts Christ above culture, a church may begin to heavily criticize the culture for its racism, sexism, or militarism (if the church is liberal or Mennonite), or the culture's acquiescence to pornography, homosexuality, and abortion (if the church is conservative). The common theme is that the culture is corrupt, and the church needs to take a strong stance against the corruption.

Christ Transforming Culture

Calvinist Christians who seek to purify culture by enhancing its best elements and offering models of Christianized culture (music, education, literature, social policy) reflect this viewpoint. The goal of the church is to bring every aspect of life under the lordship of Christ.

Adapting Niebuhr's model, let's take an ecclesiastical journey to see how twentieth century churches understand Christ in relation to the culture in which they live. The following is no detailed study but rather fleeting impressions, to show how three different churches have built their own bridges between the biblical vision of the church and the visible institutions on earth.

An Underground Church in East Germany

Some years ago Craig, a graduate student in Europe visiting Berlin, learned of a student Christian conference in the Eastern (then Communist) sector of the city. He was curious to see what sort of a witness Christian students might have under the watchful eye of a blatantly hostile regime, and so he decided to attend. There his worst fears were realized. The speakers, while obviously committed, uniformly seemed to lack any vision of the impact they could have for Christ within their own culture.

Upon leaving, Craig expressed his dismay to the conference leader and was surprised to receive an immediate invitation for coffee later that evening. At the stated hour, Craig arrived to find a nondescript, dimly lit flat. But inside were a dozen or so vibrant Christians full of joy, enthusiasm, and delight at the opportunity for fellowship with an American Christian student. They hastened to explain that government spies had infiltrated the conference; therefore the speakers could say nothing in their remarks that would have aroused suspicion. They were as unhappy as Craig at the stunted witness earlier in the evening.

Over the next two years Craig formed a friendship with the harassed students, even helping many of them to escape through the underground to freedom in the West.

Like the early Christians who met clandestinely in the catacombs of Rome during periods of persecution, the East German students knew themselves to be despised outcasts in an alien, unremittingly hostile world. Like all believers in similar circumstances, they were profoundly aware that the gospel forced them to be "against" the culture in which they lived.

Clearly, there are times and places when the church must of necessity adopt the catacomb model, but not always. The world *is* a hostile place and needs the church in her midst as salt, to keep it from being as bad as it could, and as light, to keep it from being engulfed in its own darkness. However, Jesus said that, although His people should expect persecution, such opposition should not lead to a private piety. Rather, His followers should penetrate society with a radical kind of caring and a bold kind of proclamation. The church is the body of Christ *in the world,* not in hiding.

Those of us who live in Western democracies have our own temptations to adopt a catacomb model. Whenever the church fails to be visible and to relate in loving witness and service to the world, it hides its lamp under a bushel. One of the tragedies of the modern Western church, says Lesslie Newbigin, is that it has enjoyed being a permitted and even priviledged minority so long that it has accepted being relegated to the private sphere. As a result, the power has been lost to address a radical challenge to modern Western civilization.[5] The church must rediscover its call to be salt and light.

A Cardinal Parish in Lisbon

In the old city of Lisbon, Portugal, many churches serve the teeming population crammed into narrow, picturesque streets. The Church of Saõ Carlo in particular, standing across a small square from the National Theatre, impresses tourists with its grand baroque facade. A step inside Saō Carlo, however, creates quite a different impression. Candles and statues everywhere show that the church is still a place of prayer for both residents and tourists; a handful of old women in black dresses with shawls over their heads are engrossed in meditation. But the walls are dark with soot from a huge fire which engulfed the sanctuary some years ago. Light filters through an inadequate, corrugated tin roof that lets in rain, smog, and noise from the streets outside.

Saō Carlo stands as a symbol of the tragic state of much European Christianity. In churches like her, Christ was once proclaimed above culture. When theology was seen as the queen of the sciences, and kings and queens bowed to the authority of the church, Europe recognized the church's right to dictate standards in art, music, and above all, morals. But the Constantinian church, the church which flourished in the West following legalization under Constantine in A.D. 312, is now, like Saō Carlo, an empty shell of the past.

Whether in conservative Catholic or liberal Protestant form, the chief mark of the Constantinian church has been a presumption of the right to tell society how to conform to the standards of Jesus Christ. But historic influence carries weight no longer, and society seems not to want to listen. Churches that still operate on this model forget the central biblical image of the church as the people of God called to bear witness to the power of the risen Christ. We are God's own people, said Peter, "a peculiar people," a "people for God's own posses-sion" (1 Peter 2:9 NASB). The crumbling Constantin-ian church, still visible throughout the Western world, has forgotten that while Christ is Lord over all, He will only reign when believers, brought to personal submission to Him as Lord, acknowledge Christ's kingship.

The Christ of the conforming church is a Christ of culture.

The real legacy of Constantinian thinking, say two Duke University professors, Hauerwas and Wil-limon, is no longer a greatly influential church, but rather an all-powerful modern state.[6] After all, the welfare state can now provide society with many of those things for which they once looked to the Constantinian church—and without the doctrine of hell!

Impeccability in Gibraltar

The third church in this survey is the stately An-glican cathedral in Gibraltar. On a hot Easter Sun-day morning, well-dressed gentlemen and ladies in brightly colored dresses try to keep themselves cool with fans. Lovely flowers decorate the altar, and the dean and his assistant clergy move through the liturgy with grace, alacrity, and impeccable Oxford accents. The sermon, prefaced by the announcement of a sherry party to follow in the Cathedral garden, lasts no more than seven minutes and consists mostly of greetings, a comment on the Resurrection theme portrayed in the huge rose window over the east end, and a lofty quote from a poem or two. Afterward, at the door, the provost notices an Oxford University tie and chats amiably about his years "up at Oriel." The worshipers retreat to their hotel, unmoved, unenlightened, and unchallenged.

In this brief experience in Gibraltar is found the conforming church. It was, of course, a conforming church that welcomed Hitler in Germany, for the conforming church is able to accommodate to almost any society. Today this model is at work among those who want to bring the sexual revolution into the churches; those who ordain practicing homosexuals and advocate that life-style, those who officially bless same sex unions or temporary "love" relationships, and those who replace God the Father with more "nurturing," feminine images in the liturgy and the Bible.

Nor are so-called liberal churches the only ones prone to this type of conformity. Consider the worldliness of much conservative Christianity: the slick Madison Avenue techniques used to raise funds, the adulation of sports heroes who give personal witness to their faith, and the obsession with size and numerical growth. All of this is simply accommodation to materialistic values.[7] The church strives to become culturally acceptable rather than bringing the culture under radical critique.[8] The Christ of the conforming church is a Christ *of* culture. Dean Inge said, "He who marries the spirit of the age, will become a widower in the next." The conforming church solves this problem simply by marrying again.

The conforming church forgets another key New Testament description of the church: Saints! Again and again Paul writes to the saints who are at Philippi, Colossae, and Corinth. These saints were not, of course, men and women with little halos over their heads but ordinary people who knew they had been called to be different—that is, to be holy. The conforming church, so concerned to be inclusive, pleads that because the church is a gathering of fellow sinners, we should accept each other as we are and forget this call to holiness.[9] But as John Stott argues, God's acceptance of us must never negate the need for repentance: "His 'acceptance' means that he fully and freely forgives all who repent and believe, not that he condones our continuance in sin."[10] Acceptance of one another is only as fellow penitents and fellow pilgrims, not as fellow sinners who are resolved to persist in sin. If we harden our hearts against God's Word and will, there is no acceptance, only judgment. One form that this judgment takes is for the church to become irrelevant and die. Do we really think that a church that accepts sodomy will have anything to tell most practicing sodomites? The acceptance of sin by the church of God is a shortcut to irrelevance, for the gospel has no power to save when it ceases to challenge the world at the point of sin.

Neither the catacomb church, the Constantinian

church, nor the conforming church are ideal models for today. However much some of these churches may still occasionally grab the headlines, they have lost touch with what it means to be the church in the world. The assumptions about the relationship between Christ and culture are no longer adequate for our time. Let's now ponder three other churches.

A Dump in Luanda

On a visit to the People's Republic of Angola to speak at a conference of African pastors, I stopped over for two days in the nation's capital, Luanda. Once a tourist mecca on the African Riviera, with a palm-lined promenade reminiscent of southern France, this sultry African city is home to thousands of refugees from the nation's fifteen years of civil war.[11] The streets are dusty and filled with trash. The windows of all the schools are broken. Masses huddle in high-rise apartments without plumbing. The stench of sewage permeates the foul-smelling urban air. Staples for survival are purchased at outrageous prices on the black market.

The United Nations is promising to build low-cost housing on the town dump, where rats run about as freely as the ill-clad children who call it home. But until that happy day comes, those who live in the cardboard or mud huts which cover this tree-less mound of clay can rarely afford enough tin for even a makeshift roof.

But the church is here.

Come with me. It is Sunday, and an assortment

of people speaking several languages gathers inside four cement block walls. The music begins. A line of ten fine-looking young men in ill-fitting, secondhand tweed jackets and unmatching ties march in, praising the Lord with a lovely antiphon in a tribal language. There are no instruments, but the sound fills the air with beauty. Onlookers join in. A preacher expounds God's Word; the sermon is translated from Umbundu into Portuguese, then quietly into French, and finally English. Earnest prayers are said. Smiles greet the stranger from North America. I am invited to say a word and am warmly thanked for my presence.

This is a confessing church. Here in Angola is a church who knows that the relationship between Christ and culture must be one of mission. The believers are profoundly aware that they are the "new creation" spoken of in Scripture.[12] Saved from drugs, thievery, prostitution, and hopelessness, these new believers are the hope of Luanda.

And they are not alone. All over the city, congregations like this little one are bearing witness to the fact that a new world is coming. These African churches, growing by leaps and bounds, do not need to be told that the nineties are the decade of evangelism. Evangelism is at the heart of their life. The Christ whom they have experienced is sending them out into their cultures as witnesses by word and deed with the confidence that He will build His church "and the gates of Hades shall not prevail against it" (Matt. 16:18).[13]

A Cave in Jerusalem

Come with me now to Jerusalem—the Jerusalem of the 1960s. Divided as always by bitterness between Jews and Arabs, the Holy City endures a tense coexistence made possible by armed sentinels and a barren "no man's land" separating the Israeli and Jordanian sectors.

As a student tourist, I am being shown the oldest part of the city, overlooking the Kidron Valley to the south and east. My guide, Ahid, an Arab, is very friendly. Later I will go to his house to meet his family. But for now I am staring over a wall, looking down at a group of caves far below. Figures are moving slowly in and out of the rocky caverns which, I am told, serve as homes for the homeless. I ask Ahid who these homeless people are.

"Lepers," he replies. "There is a leper colony down there. They are so poor and unwanted that they must live in caves."

"But who are those in black moving among them?" I ask.

"They are Moravian missionaries," says Ahid, "Christian women who tend the lepers and feed them."

I stare for a long time at the pathetic sight, wondering about the motivations of those women, wondering what they have given up, wondering at the risks they were taking. Then I realize that I am seeing the caring church at work. I am seeing the church who has not forgotten that Jesus took a towel, washed His disciples' feet, and told them to do the same. Here is a church who knows that the relationship between Christ and culture must be one of service: Christ for culture.

One of the biblical images for the church is "servants of God." William Barclay calls this the "proudest title for the church in the Bible."[14] The Greek word for servant was *doulos,* meaning "slave." By using this word the New Testament church acknowledged her Lord's absolute right to loving obedience, claimed no rights of her own, and professed the ultimate goal of living for the pleasure of Christ (see Phil. 1:1). To modern ears this sounds demeaning, but the role of servanthood was freely (even proudly) accepted by believers. Service was not dutiful bondage but rather "perfect freedom."[15]

A Hall in Mexico City

Finally, come with me to Mexico City in late December in 1957. I am twenty years old, wandering around the streets by myself, feeling miserable because my immediate family is coming apart at the seams and all the familiar props are being pulled out from under me. I have no clear vision of the future and am struggling with the meaning of faith and commitment.

With a day and a night to kill before my plane leaves, I can find no solace in the great cathedrals of Mexico City. They are grim, dusty, crumbling fortresses witnessing to a bygone era of colonial grandeur. Besides, they are largely empty, although I see one man in a business suit, his face distorted by pain, crawling on his knees across an immense pavement on his way into church. Doubtless he is on his way up to the high altar as an act of penance for sin. I wonder to myself, is that the way of Christ?

The evening falls quickly in December and I need something to do to pass the time. Just then I see, in a brightly lit hall, a crowd of people sitting on rows of benches, singing. I decide to go in and pray silently in a back pew. Hands wave here and there during the music until a woman preacher walks to the podium. She begins to preach to her simple but zealous congregation. Words tumble out of her mouth with an intensity that mark her as an evangelist, and there is fire in her eyes. I feel at peace in that place, sitting there among strangers in that foreign city at Christmas time. Although I know virtually no Spanish, a single phrase catches my attention.

"It is finished." The work of Christ on the cross is finished. There is no more to be done but believe, give thanks, and praise. No more sacrifices, no more penance, no more pleadings . . . it is finished. Somehow, all this is communicated through one or two words in a language I do not understand. But the message comes through loud and clear. I leave refreshed, thankful, at peace.

That little church in Mexico City is an image of the centered church—the church that is centered on the mighty acts of God in Christ: His Cross, His Resurrection, and His sending of the Spirit. The contrast with elaborate cathedrals couldn't be greater. But, as Luther wrote: "The church's holiness does not consist in surplices, tonsures, long clerical gowns, and other ceremonies ... fabricated without the warrant of Holy Writ; but in God's Word and true faith."[16]

So here in Luanda, Jerusalem, and Mexico City can be found three models of the church: The confessing church, the caring church, and the Christ-centered church. Each model outlines a distinct understanding of the relationship between Christ and culture: Christ to culture (the confessing church, emphasizing mission); Christ for culture (the caring church, emphasizing compassion); and Christ completing culture (the centered church, emphasizing the proclamation of the Word).

What is not to be found in Scripture or in the Creed is Christ apart from culture. There is no model for the Christian who thinks that he or she can be a solitary follower, staking out a spiritual life apart from the family of God, relying on personal piety and resourcefulness to make it through. Neither the sports enthusiast who "finds God" on the golf course, nor the recluse who shuns Christian fellowship are acceptable models from the New Testament point of view.

Henri Nouwen makes an interesting case for the Desert Fathers (and Mothers) who retreated from civilization to live in the Egyptian desert in the fourth and fifth centuries. Once official persecution of Christians had died down, he says, these rigorous Christians sought a way to express a radical and costly Christian commitment in the light of the world's infiltration of the church.[17] But Jesus never specifically recommended that kind of radical separation from the world in Scripture. His retreats from the crowd were periodic, and his only lengthy period of solitude was to wrestle with Satan for forty days before beginning His public ministry (see Matt. 4:1–11).

There is no model for the Christian who thinks that he or she can be a solitary follower.

The images God gives of the church in the New Testament are all corporate: "new Israel," "household," "ambassadors," "exiles," "flock," "brethren," "friends," "disciples," "branches." Only as believers are united to Christ and to one another in a life of faith and accountability is there hope of avoiding the tragedy of assimilation by the world. That is why the story of the Swiss Family Robinson is inherently more believable than the story of Robinson Crusoe. In Johann Wyss' tale, a family operating in love and faith together tamed the jungle and lived to tell the story. The individual washed up alone on a desert island can lose the power of speech or ultimately, of life.

Questions for Discussion

1. Does your church confess belief in the "catholic" church? Discuss the validity of using or not using that word.

2. Is privatism a characteristic of your church today?

3. How should the church critique aesthetic standards in art and music in our culture? What about standards of morality?

4. How inclusive do you think the church should be? What is the place for church discipline?

5. If you could spend a day with the Christians of Luanda, the Moravians of Jerusalem, or the Pentecostals of Mexico City, which would you choose and why?

Finger in the Sand

The forgiveness of sins

The autumn leaves of the Massachusetts countryside beckoned students to Clear Hill on sunny Sunday afternoons. Dominated by a tall water tower, the remote place was favored by teenage lawbreakers from the boarding school I was attending. One Sunday, a group of schoolmates and I slipped away to share a pack of Camels at the forbidden spot. I sat with the crowd, a silent accomplice trying desperately to fit in, but feeling decidedly ill at ease because of my high regard for school rules. I declined to smoke.

At fifteen I was certainly not above doing forbidden things. I could have come up with as spicy a litany of youthful infractions as anyone. However, that day I felt an outsider. "Why is it," I was wondering, "that when people are forbidden to do something, they so desperately want to do it?"

Had I known then of Augustine's *Confessions* I might have compared my actions to his, when he and his friends, for no apparent reason, decided to steal pears from a neighbor's orchard to throw to the hogs. "Such was my heart, God . . . It would engage in wrongdoing for no reason or provocation, and sin just for the fun of sinning." Reflecting on his senseless action, Augustine pondered:

What was it about the pear theft that appealed to unhappy fifteen-year-old me? To be quite honest, this little act of mine did not even have the enticing, shady, counterfeit kind of charm that vice so often uses to deceive us. I loved it because of the companionship of the fellows with whom I did it. If I had loved the pears I made off with, and wanted to enjoy them, I might have stolen them all by myself. Obviously the fun did not come from the pears! My pleasure was not in *what* I stole, but *that* I stole. Our chief pleasure was derived from the knowledge that we had done what was forbidden.[1]

A Dark Cloud Over Life

I returned to school later that afternoon and sought the comfort of my older brother's room. We talked carelessly about the incident and the questions it had raised in my mind. He asked just who had been involved and I told him.

But my brother was a monitor, one of the select

group of seven seniors who "ran" the school. Before I knew what had happened, my older brother—with that high sense of duty common to firstborns—proceeded to turn the other boys in. A crisis ensued. The boys were summoned to the headmaster's study to face a stern reprimand. Letters were written to parents. It is a wonder they were not expelled, for in those strict days boys had been asked to leave for lesser offenses. For several weeks, a cloud hung over that campus of two hundred adolescent boys.

Tongues, of course, began to wag. It did not take long for the others to figure out how information had been leaked to the authorities. One afternoon, I opened my door to find a delegation of the biggest, toughest bruisers in the class ahead of me demanding an explanation. I tried my best to remain calm, told the truth, and assured them that I had not intended to rat on them. Then something quite amazing happened: They believed me! To this day I cannot explain why, but despite the unfavorable consequences they had received, the upperclassmen decided that I was "okay."

My own class was quite a different story. Those who had been implicated were angry and resentful. They refused to accept an explanation. Months later—long after I thought the dust had settled—I asked one of those I considered a friend, if he had forgiven me. His reply stung: "I will never forgive you."

I lived in the tension of those two conflicting attitudes for the rest of my high school career. The vividness of the experience has remained with me as a living reminder of the difference between being and not being forgiven.

The Door That Opens Both Ways

In His teaching Jesus forbade any separation of God's forgiveness of us from our forgiveness of others: "Forgive us our debts, as we forgive our debtors" (Matt. 6:12). Jesus was saying that the door to the realm of forgiveness must open both ways. God's forgiveness and our forgiveness of one another are inextricably linked. I cannot be forgiven if, at the same time, I refuse to forgive. For Jesus, there were two contrasting realms: the realm of forgiveness and the realm of alienation. In the former, mercy transcends simple justice. If rules are broken, there is forgiveness, to be received but also to be passed on. In the realm of alienation, simple justice is applied: Break the rules, suffer the consequences. Compensation comes in the form of self-righteousness, inflicting consequences on others when they break the rules.

When we choose Christ—or rather, are chosen by Him—we enter the realm of forgiveness. To choose against Christ is to choose the realm of alienation. M. Scott Peck describes this simple but serious choice as the difference between heaven and hell: "There are only two states of being: submission to God and goodness or the refusal to submit to anything beyond one's own will—which refusal automatically enslaves one to the forces of evil. We must ultimately belong either to God or the devil."[2]

The Nicene Creed explicitly links baptism and forgiveness with the words: "I believe in one baptism for the remission of sins." In the Apostles' Creed, the linkage is implicit. Because the Apostles' Creed is a baptismal creed, the assumption is that once a convert's past is laid to rest in the waters of baptism, the future will be an exemplary life. However, as the world, the flesh and the devil have pressed in upon the church in history, some believers have fallen quite badly—even to the point of renouncing Christ under the pressure of persecution. The question of how to handle these lapsed believers poses quite a problem, particularly because tough statements like those in Hebrews (6:4–6; 10:26) and 1 John (5:16) imply that serious postconversion sin puts one beyond the realm of help.

**The door to forgiveness
must open both ways.**

Why would the early church have had such difficulty with tolerance for the "backslider"? Apparently, the realization was painful for Christians that not all were willing to pay the price for discipleship that the first apostles (to say nothing of Jesus Himself) had had to pay. The concern was not simple self-righteousness. In the pre-Constantinian era, "nominal Christianity" was not an acceptable alternative to serious commitment; hence the question of forgiveness for a fallen believer who wished to return was a crisis that had to be faced. The ease with which modern believers are prepared to forgive their own sins—even to view them "minor personal foibles"—would have appeared very strange to early Christians.

At stake were two different understandings of the church. Was the church a gathering of saints, where serious infractions were grounds for exclusion from the body, or a hospital for sinners, where people are always welcomed back? This exclusive/inclusive tension is the same that exists in our own day.

Forgiveness frees people from the spiral of revenge and resentment so that the course of justice can begin.

Efforts to bring together a high view of baptism with the need to forgive those who had fallen into serious sins after baptism plunged the early church into controversy. Certain sins, such as adultery, homicide, and apostasy were deemed particularly serious. But by the third century a compassionate attitude, appreciative of human frailty and in tune with the spirit of the Gospels, was steadily gaining ground. "The Christian ideal that baptism ought to be the one and only penance is amply recognized ... at the same time the bishop is exhorted to reconcile all repentant sinners." A Syrian document from the period describes the bishop sitting in the church as a judge, appointed by God and charged by God with the power of binding and loosing. The people are to view his authority as from high; and he is to be "loved like a father, feared like a king and honoured as God."[3]

Forgiveness vs. Justice

Contemporary challenge to the view of the church as a place for sinners comes from Christian-Marxist dialogue. Marxists scorn the Christian doctrine of forgiveness. To place emphasis on the forgiveness of sin renders impotent the struggle with evil. In their zeal to restructure society along egalitarian lines, Marxists see the willingness of the oppressed to forgive their oppressors as a weakening of their case and an encouragement to a passive attitude about oppression. Forgiveness blurs the lines of division in the class struggle and "leads to a sentimental concealment of the real clash of interests between exploited and the exploiters, and to a premature reconciliation with unforgivable conditions."[4]

Marxists do have a point. Sometimes the church, in encouraging forgiveness, has not taken the second necessary, but often risky, step of challenging oppressors. The church has at times made oppressors welcome in Jesus' name without doing what Jesus did—confronting the rationalizations of sin and demanding justice. But the Marxist critique fails to understand the true nature of Christian forgiveness. Far from obliterating justice, forgiveness frees people from the spiral of revenge and resentment so that the course of justice can begin. One has only to think of Zacchaeus, an arch-capitalist. Jesus eats with him, but by the time He is done, Zacchaeus has decided to give up being a publican and a sinner, and wants to restore several times over the money he has swindled (see Luke 19:1–10). Mercy fulfills justice because justice by nature is full of compassionate concern for the whole spectrum of human needs—spiritual and psychological as well as economic. The gospel refuses to see people only as *homo-economicus.*

Forgiveness never excuses the wrongdoer.

In a moving account of the conversion of Alexander Solzhenitsyn in a Siberian prison during Stalin's reign of terror, Charles Colson tells of the embittered Jewish doctor from whom the Nobel Prize-winning author learned of Christ. Dr. Boris Kornfeld was deeply sensitive to the suffering of his fellow Jews under successive Russian rulers over the centuries. There in prison, disillusioned with socialism, he heard from a fellow prisoner of a suffering Messiah who came as a Jew for Jews to suffer, die, and bring hope and salvation. Kornfeld was especially moved by the Lord's Prayer, and said it often: "Forgive us our sins, as we forgive those who sin against us."

Boris Kornfeld became a Christian and his life began to change. As a prison doctor he was in an ideal position to take vengeance upon his captors, many of whom were patients, and in the past he had often plotted to do so. Now, he was meticulous in treating them justly. This fairness eventually brought him into conflict with the orderlies, who in return for special favors, acted as informants for the guards. Kornfeld was killed one night in his operating room, presumably by these orderlies, but not before he had shared the excitement over his newfound faith with a patient. The patient was Solzhenitsyn; and he lived to tell the world Kornfeld's story.[5]

The Cross or the Circle

Justice demands that forgiveness mean more than simply accepting the sinner. It begins with a frank admission that the sin is a deliberate transgression of God's justice. The next crucial step is to acknowledge that God has condemned the wrongdoer, but He offers reconciliation under the Cross. Forgiveness never excuses the wrongdoer but confronts sin honestly. There is no place for euphemisms like: "He couldn't help running the boy down because he had a drinking problem—we all have to try and understand."

The symbol of Christianity is the cross, where conflict leads to reconciliation. Other religions attempt to offer peace but they deny the fundamental conflict between good and evil. The circle, for instance, is the symbol favored in Hindu and Buddhist spirituality as a unifying principle in the world. Ken Wilber, who writes critically of the boundaries which divide, separate, and alienate, speaks of a unifying consciousness which, like the ripples in a pond, moves out in all directions, eventually enfolding everything, the good and the evil, the illusory and the real, the pleasure and the pain.[6] But this minimizing of sin only reflects a lack of interest in the sufferings of others. The often-heard adage, "forgive and forget," also runs the risk of turning defective memory into a virtue.

When individuals refuse to join with the body in Holy Communion for whatever reason, they excommunicate themselves.

Christian forgiveness involves the deliberate turning from the painful memories of life to face the full light of God's holy love. Only at the Cross are the demands of God's justice that evil be treated as evil met and overcome. Only there does God's love reach out to embrace sinners. At that point, Christianity does not just *include* forgiveness, it *is* forgiveness. As Karl Barth wrote: "The forgiveness of sins is the basis, the sum, the criterion of all that can be called Christian life or Christian faith."[7]

Holy Inclusiveness

The special unity which the Cross brings is demonstrated principally by the Lord's table at Holy Communion. Here is inclusiveness in spite of sin, rather than inclusiveness ignorant of sin. In the church which I serve this is vividly symbolized by an oval communion rail which completely surrounds the Holy Table. People kneel together around the signs of Christ's body and blood to receive in community the bread and wine. All remain until all receive.

All Christians recognize the table of the Lord as the place symbolizing unity. It is not by saying a creed, singing hymns, or by joining with one another in projects and programs that unity is demonstrated. At the foot of the Cross, eating the Lord's body and drinking His blood by faith, in the forms of bread and wine, we are bound together. This is why excommunication, separation from the very sphere where forgiveness is made tangible, is such a drastic act and so rarely used. This is also why, when individuals refuse to join with the body in Holy Communion for whatever reason, they excommunicate themselves. We are only members of that body with which we are prepared to go to the Lord's table. The ancient tradition of "passing the peace" means more than merely saying "hello" to the next person in the pew. Passing the peace symbolizes our readiness to be reconciled with our brother and sister, to forgive and to be forgiven.

Finger in the Sand

In the well-known story of Jesus and the woman taken in adultery, much speculation has centered on what Jesus wrote in the sand.[8] As John tells it, a married woman, caught *in flagrante delicto,* dragged from her lover's bed and thrown like a heap of garbage at the feet of Jesus, is justly condemned by the leaders of the church. According to the Law of Moses she should have been stoned. However, the Scribes and Pharisees had no intention of seeing that happen.[9] For one thing, they could not exercise the power of capital punishment. That rested with Rome. Their goal was for Jesus to incriminate Himself by openly declaring that He disagreed with the Law of Moses. They were quite aware that if Jesus sided with Moses and approved her execution, He would ruin His reputation for compassion among the people. Alternatively, if He argued for leniency He would appear to be lax regarding the Law. Thrusting this situation on Jesus, suddenly and publicly, they hoped in one way or another to discredit His ministry.

They said to Jesus, "Now Moses, in the law, commanded us that such should be stoned. But what do you say?" Jesus chose to ignore their question. Bending down, He began to write with His finger in the sand. But just what did He write? Some ancient commentators have thought he wrote the seventh commandment: "Thou shalt not commit adultery," as if to say: "Why ask Me? It is written in the Law. The Law which God wrote with His finger, as I am doing now." Other commentators think that He wrote Jeremiah 17:13: "Those who depart from Me shall be written in the earth," as if to say: "You Scribes and Pharisees have forsaken My way of forgiveness and you shall be exposed in shame." One commentator even offers the unlikely suggestion that Jesus could not look at the woman, He was so ashamed of her and of the story He had been told. Many in recent years, though, have followed Calvin, who said that Jesus wasn't writing anything in particular but was only doodling.[10]

Perhaps Jesus was taking the time to think of what He would say. It is likely that adultery was not the real issue but rather reconciling the vision of God given through Moses ("whoever touches the mountain—man or beast—shall surely be put to death") with His own revolutionary teaching of God as the Forgiving Father of the Prodigal Son. The Pharisees' question was entirely legitimate (their methods may be another story). They knew that if Jesus could not come up with a good answer, there was no reason why people should believe that He was from God.[11]

So then, as Jesus pondered His answer, He invited the one who was without sin to cast the first stone. The Pharisees were skewered. They all fell silent. Which one could claim total purity in thought and deed? One by one, from the eldest to the youngest (the youngest having the hottest heads and therefore the greatest indignation), they left. At this point the story reads: "Jesus was left alone with the woman standing *in the midst*." The Greek is very clear: they were alone, but in the midst. In the midst of what? In the midst of the crowd which had gathered, in the midst of all the sympathetic onlookers who had been watching the whole confrontation. Who, then, had gone away? The circle of condemning people—that gathering of self-righteous saints who, although they had justice on their side, had no heart for forgiveness. But, while the inner circle had vanished, the outer crowd of the multitude was still present. Within earshot of them, Jesus then said: "'Woman, where are those accusers of yours? Has no one condemned you?' She said, 'No one, Lord.' And Jesus said to her, 'Neither do I condemn you; go and sin no more'" (John 8:9–11).

William Barclay, whose comments on the Gospels are otherwise quite illuminating, surprisingly says that Jesus was giving the woman another chance to prove herself![12] By thinking Jesus was putting the woman on a kind of probation, Barclay seems to miss the point. The woman experienced all that those who come to Jesus in their shame experience.[13] She was taken from the courtroom of the law, into the throne room of grace. She discovered what it means not to be condemned; and in the freedom of that non-condemning presence she found the grace to change. Nor does that grace obliterate justice. Justice is served—not by the strict implementation of the law, but rather by the transformed behavior of a woman, now forgiven, set free from the guilt and power of her sin.

O Felix Culpa! (O Happy Guilt!)

Although the modern mind would like to brush aside the idea of sin, the issue is critical. We confess our faith in the "forgiveness of sins." Without sin we are left without responsibility; and without responsibility, we are without the moral capacity for change. The idea of sin enables us to separate the wrongdoer as a person from his or her wrongdoing as an act. True sin originates in the heart, as Jesus said, but so does repentance and renewal.

Even the widely misunderstood Reformation doctrine of total depravity never implied that there was nothing good anywhere in the person. It said that there was no area of a person's life untouched by sin. There is "no health (or wholeness) in us," as the confession in the *Book of Common Prayer* puts it. Paul distinguished his *self* from his *sin*. Caught in the struggle with sin that every believer striving to change knows all too well, Paul says: "If then, I do what I will not to do . . . it is no longer I who do it, but sin that dwells in me." Instead of lightening Paul's responsibility, this clear focus on the seriousness of sin gives him hope for change: "Who will deliver me from this body of death? I thank God—through Jesus Christ our Lord!" (Rom. 7:16, 17, 24, 25).

God's forgiveness is both compassionate and creative. He removes from our shoulders the weight of condemnation, and by that very fact creates the conditions for moral change and justice-making. As Helmut Thielicke says, forgiveness does not so much mean that I am chemically cleansed, but "rather that my sin no longer separates me from God, that it can no longer be a chasm that cuts me off from the Father."[14] I now long to please the God whom I had wounded by my sin.

But we must never think that forgiveness is cheap. The shadow of the Cross falls on all forgiveness, both God's and ours. That which cost God the pain of total rejection will cost us also, at the very least, some faint reflection of Calvary. Forgiveness is "bloody." Years ago as a university student I entered a church one Ash Wednesday evening in search of a quiet Communion service. The nonliturgical Protestant service was already underway when I slipped in at the back. I listened carefully to the unfamiliar words and noticed no confession of sin and no absolution. Then I realized that there was no mention of the Cross or the Resurrection. Even the bread and the wine were devoid of biblical meaning. The loaf of bread, said the minister, symbolized our oneness, and the cup symbolized our shared pain and joy.

I remember being so profoundly disturbed that, as the people filed forward, I decided to leave. Making my way to the door, I wondered what that cozy circle of people was doing. What did that service have to do with those two intersecting lines where, on Calvary's cross, God clashed with human injustice and, out of His blood and pain, brought forgiveness and joy to the world?

Repentance

We must beware of trying to enter the realm of forgiveness in a halfhearted way. Only genuine repentance opens us to forgiveness—a repentance that freely recognizes what part we have played to make the world more wicked, forsakes vengeance, and is willing to make amends where necessary.

The pardon of Richard Nixon by President Ford illustrates the danger of severing forgiveness from repentance. Nixon neither openly admitted guilt nor showed signs of repentance; yet Ford's "pardon" itself implied guilt, as did Nixon's acceptance of it. The whole charade left the ex-President more alienated than before from the nation he had served. Had there been some confession, some signs of genuine repentance, many Americans, if not all, would have forgiven him. Lem Hubbard in the *Chicago Tribune* once said: "In the sphere of forgiveness, too many hatchets are buried alive." That is, too many people have *officially* buried the hatchet but have *unofficially* no intention of leaving it there. In the words of Jeremiah, they have "healed the hurt of the daughter of My peoples lightly, saying, 'Peace, peace!' when there is no peace" (8:11).

Those who find forgiveness too costly discover to their sadness that it is not nearly as costly as its opposite: an unforgiving spirit. Those who will not forgive eventually become imprisoned by their own bitterness, which is a double victory for those who wounded them in the first place.

After confessing our faith week by week in "the

forgiveness of sins," Christians try to walk side by side as reconciled, forgiven sinners. Together we draw fresh strength from God's table to live the new life God has called us to. There is no need to shrink from Holy Communion or wait until we feel worthy, for the worthiness is not in ourselves but in the One who waits to feed us. Nor is the worthiness of the sacrament in the celebrant, the minister.[15] The effect of the sacrament depends not on human worthiness at all, but on the gospel it dramatizes, which we appropriate through faith.

The story is told that C. S. Lewis arrived late for a convention of theologians who had been discussing for hours the issue: Where is Christianity distinctive? What Christian doctrine has no parallel in any of the other religions in the world? When Lewis heard of the dispute, and of the inability of the theologians to come to an answer, he calmly said, "That's easy: the forgiveness of sins."[16]

Opening the Door

Reader, have you moved from the realm of condemnation to the realm of forgiveness? Have you left the courtroom of the law and entered the throne room of grace? Are you set free from the simple and distorted justice of the world to be reconciled to your enemy and to begin the process of making true justice to the glory of God? In the moving words of George Herbert, a seventeenth century British poet, let me invite you to make that all-important change. Drop your resentment toward

God or your bitterness toward that person against whom you have a case so airtight that even God should understand it, and let Christ welcome you into His new and glorious realm:

> Love bade me welcome; yet my soul drew back,
>   Guilty of dust and sin.
> But quick-eyed Love, observing me grow slack
>   From my first entrance in,
> Drew nearer to me, sweetly questioning,
>   If I lacked anything.
>
> "A guest," I answered, "worthy to be here."
>   Love said, "You shall be he."
> "I, the unkind, ungrateful? Ah, my dear,
>   I cannot look on thee."
> Love took my hand, and smiling did reply,
>   "Who made the eyes but I?"
>
> "Truth, Lord, but I have marred them; let my shame
>   Go where it doth deserve."
> "And know you not," says Love, "who bore the
>   blame?"
>   "My dear, then I will serve."
> "You must sit down," says Love, "and taste my
>   meat."
>   So I did sit and eat.[17]

Questions for Discussion

1. Jeremiah said, "The heart is deceitful above all things, and desperately wicked; who can know it?" (17:9). Do you agree?

2. Do you, in some sense, "earn" forgiveness by forgiving others?

3. What is the "unforgiveable sin"? See Matthew 12:31–32.

4. Is the church you attend more like a "museum for saints" or a "hospital for sinners"?

5. Why could Augustine say *"O felix culpa,"* (O happy guilt)?

Unfinished Symphony

The resurrection of the body, and the life everlasting

Geoff seemed to be a pleasant, respectful, artic-ulate university student from Canada, taking a semester at the University of Lausanne to brush up on his French. But over tea and cake in our apartment one afternoon, my wife and I soon real-ized that Geoff's outgoing personality masked a profound pessimism, evident on almost every page of the loose-leaf volume of poetry he eagerly shared with us. The themes of suicide, death, loneliness, and emptiness ran through several of his poems. One struck me as particularly sad:

> *I was, once, a little boy—*
> *Running free—full of joy.*
>
> *I was, once, a young man—*
> *Running—along the sand.*

I was, once, an elder man—
Standing—by the sea, in the sand.

I was, once . . .

At that time of life, I had not yet learned that the major transitions of life are often accompanied by a sense of loss and anxiety over death.[1] Geoff's transition from high school student to university, coupled with his estrangement in a foreign country would naturally lead to a sense of grief over the symbolic death of the youth he once was.

At the time of such life transitions, people are often willing to talk about death and the possibility of life beyond the grave. Without meaning, hope, and a sense of purpose, they may choose to succumb to the despair they feel inside. Such may be a cause of the soaring rise in suicide statistics within the past thirty years.[2] Those who do not actually take their own lives, may simply lose the will to live. Howard Hughes, the multimillionaire entrepreneur, died in middle adulthood of starvation, disease, and emotional isolation. Daniel J. Levinson writes: "He could invest his money with great profit, but he could not invest his self in any enterprise or obtain psychic income from it. He finally suffocated within the cocoon he had built around himself."[3]

The Great Denial

Most people, however, attempt to deal with death by denial. Some look to science; others look to philosophy or religion. But the quest for immortality has become big business whichever way you slice the cake. Imagine, for a moment, that there existed an early childhood vaccine to prevent hereditary diseases. The vaccine would protect one's system from future causes of death. If such a scenario sounds like fantasy, it is not. It may be just around the corner. Today we are at the point in genetic engineering research, says *The Economist,* that the auto industry was in 1900! "Genes can be identified, weighed, measured, counted, manipulated, replicated, and mutated in test tubes, and shuttled from cell to cell, even across species barriers," says the President of the International Congress of Genetics.[4]

The quest for immortality has become big business.

In the United States alone there are six hundred biotechnology companies hard at work, trying to find ways of doing everything from choosing the color of our child's eyes to eating to our heart's content without gaining an ounce of weight! What fuels this incredible investment of money and brains in the field of biotechnology is, of course, the age-old quest for immortality.

To say that this is all bad would be churlish. Who would want to live back in the days before medical breakthroughs like penicillin or anesthesia? Nevertheless, those who look to biotechnology to solve the problem of death may be inviting more problems than society can handle. When Brenda Winners found out that her unborn child lacked most of its brain's cerebral cortex, she and her husband chose not to abort the child. They kept the child alive after birth until the organs could be harvested as transplants for others. What are the implications of this sort of decision? Might not children be conceived and brought to birth for the sole purpose of providing healthy organs for unhealthy adults? There are rumors that it is already happening. Concern over possible excesses in genetic engineering has risen to a loud protest. Washington attorney Jeremy Rifkin asks: "Who is going to make all these decisions? What right have we to tamper with the building blocks of life?"[5]

A "Nullifidian's" Faith

While some look to science, others search for a solution to death through philosophy. In his quest for an alternative to the traditional religious views about life after death, British playwright J. B. Priestley borrowed a theory from a mathematician and philosopher of the late nineteenth century named J. W. Dunne. Dunne had theorized that time, like space, is multi-dimensional. Although we sense ourselves to be traveling as if on a train, from one station to the next, from the perspective of time the whole track exists at once: past, present, and future. According to Dunne and his disciple Priestley, all living organisms are immortal and exist simultaneously, even though we experience them one by one.

Priestley decided to put this theory to the test on the London stage. *Time and the Conways,* his play in three acts, depicts an upper-middle class British family during the period from about 1919 to 1939. In the first act, a family of fun-loving young adults, their beaus, and their widowed mother frolic at a birthday party in a grand house on the outskirts of London. In the second act, the same characters are summoned back to the old house. Now some twenty years have passed, and the family has gone to seed. One child has died; another has become a stuttering buffoon, living at home and doing nothing; another has become a hardbitten headmistress; another an alcoholic. The dominant mother has turned into a tyrant.

Has all been lost? Was all the joy of yesteryear merely an illusion? In the third act Priestley takes the audience back to the birthday party which opened the play. This time, however, the viewer begins to see the invisible seeds of destruction being planted even while frivolity goes on. Priestley suggests that we are the sum of our total selves, never what we appear to be at any given time. So Alan Conway tells his sister, Kay:

> Now, at this moment, or any moment, we're only a cross-section of our real selves. What we *really* are is the whole stretch of ourselves, all our time, and when we come to the end of this life, all those selves, all our time, will be *us*—the real you, the real me.

And then perhaps we'll find ourselves in another time, which is only another kind of dream.

Kay replies: "As if we're all immortal beings?" And Alan says: "Yes, and in for a tremendous adventure."[6]

Priestley styled himself a "nullifidian"—that is, a nonbeliever. His made-up word is an oxymoron or contradiction in terms. To believe in "nothing" is, of course, to believe in something (i.e., *nothing*). In fact, Priestley is very much a believer. His theory of immortality is simply a variant of the old Greek idea of the immortality of the soul, no more capable of scientific verification than the many theories Priestley criticized.

It's Immaterial

The ancient Greeks approached the problem of death by believing that some part of us survives into eternity. The Stoics, for example, were pantheists; they believed that since everything was God, God was in everything. Our souls are sparks of the divine encased in human bodies. Hence, death is the release of the soul and its reabsorption back into the divine being from which it has come.

Many people find the idea of the immortality of the soul appealing. Even Christians have cheerfully confessed it, thinking they were standing on firm Christian ground. In a survey I once gave to my biblically literate congregation, fully eighty percent of them said that they believed in it! Because I was not trying to test their capacity for fine distinctions, I had not asked if they believed in the (distinctively Christian) idea of the "resurrection of the body." To be fair, I suppose, I should have. C. S. Lewis once pointed out that the immortality of the soul is easier to believe in than the resurrection of the body. Pantheism's world view, he argued, is always more popular than Christianity's, for while it asks people to believe in a two-storied universe, nature and supernature, it keeps these two stories quite separate.[7] Nature is clear and scientifically measurable. Supernature is vague, spiritual, undifferentiated, mystical, and beyond the powers of understanding or perception. The distinctly Christian idea that nature and supernature might someday converge in a transformed material/spiritual reality is difficult to believe—as difficult as the Incarnation.

In its purest form, the idea of the immortality of the soul is that some part of human beings is intrinsically immortal. Some Christian theologians have defended the idea of human immortality on the grounds that, through union with Christ, believers are able to share in the divine life; but most recognize an inherent conflict in the idea of human immortality because God alone has immortality (see 1 Tim. 6:16).

The idea of the immortality of the soul, in its Greek or Eastern form, raises several issues. First, it minimizes the seriousness of death. If only a part of humans die (and the flesh is not the most important part), there is no place for the sense of outrage that comes at death, even our own. Imagine telling that to a mother who has just lost a child to leukemia, or to a friend who has just been diagnosed with cancer! A denial of the horror of death means denial of the possibility of hope for the conquest of death, or for personal reunion on the far side of the grave.

Second, the immortality of the soul ultimately consigns material creation to the dungheap. To the immortalist, matter doesn't matter. Logically, then, all that is beautiful; all that is appreciable by taste, touch, smell, or sight, is in the end dispensable. What is this, if taken as a comprehensive view of the afterlife, but the final thumbs down to creativity and to the Creator?

Third, the idea of immortality of the soul obliterates individuality. What survives is not the unique creature we believe ourselves to be, but some impersonal part dissolved into the All. Everything that makes people unique, personal, knowable, in the end is lost.

A Growing Awareness

Because life is a sacred gift, spoken into reality by the Prince of Life, death is an affront to the very order of things. Death is not to be treated trivially, for it is a serious contender for the throne from whence all reality is ruled. Entropy, also called the second law of thermodynamics, is the scientific theory which says that with every expenditure of energy the universe is winding down. If indeed the universe is continuously moving toward ultimate, final disorder and death, the God we claim to know can be nothing more than what H. G. Wells called Him, the "fast fading smile of a cosmic Cheshire Cat."

The Bible's answer to the problem of death is rooted in the nature of God as Creator and Redeemer. In the Old Testament, there were only hints of life beyond the grave (see Job 19:25, 26; Ps. 17:15; 49:15; Isa. 26:19; Dan. 12:2, 13). These faint glimpses pointed to a fuller understanding yet to come.

By the time of Jesus, belief in the resurrection of the dead was firmly grounded in most Jewish thought. But the apostolic writers presented the full-orbed truth of the doctrine of the resurrection in their letters to the churches. Given new hope through Jesus' own resurrection from the dead, Peter wrote of "new heavens and a new earth" (2 Peter 3:13), John of the "holy city, New Jerusalem, coming down out of heaven" (Rev. 21:2), and Paul of a "new creation" (2 Cor. 5:17). In 1 Corinthians 15 and Romans 8 Paul said that our resurrected bodies would be free from sickness and decay, without sexual passions or procreative powers, free from sin and death, totally responsive to the Spirit, and gloriously part of the renewal of the whole of creation. With these new bodies we would be perfectly suited to the ecology of heaven.

According to these apostolic writers, two things guarantee these invisible realities: First, the dramatic reversal of death in the resurrection of Jesus, whose new life had these very properties; and second, the presence of the Holy Spirit dwelling in our physical bodies. They saw the Holy Spirit as the first installment of great things to come (see Eph. 1:14). With these two guarantees, they faced persecution, weakness, suffering, even torture because "even though our outward man is perishing, yet the inward man is being renewed day by day" (2 Cor. 4:16).

The biblical vision, then, is of a universe in which matter will one day be completely under the control of spirit—a day when the great yawning gap between matter and spirit is finally overcome.

Wearyings and Yearnings

The world into which this New Testament witness first came found the message of the Resurrection strange. Many, tired of life and jaded with the indulgences of Roman society, had given up on hope beyond the grave. Horace saw the end of life as final. Sallust quotes Caesar as saying: "beyond [death] there is no place for sorrow or for joy." Juvenal claimed that not even children in his day believed in an underworld. Pliny saw life after death as a fairy tale; and Seneca said there is simply "nothing." In a moment of sadness, Cicero said, "Not to have been born were best; the earliest possible death the next best." And Catullus, standing at his brother's grave, said, "And for ever, brother, hail and farewell."

Not all Romans, however, had abandoned hope of life beyond the grave. In addition to the Stoics, who believed that the soul survived death, at least for a time, there were thousands who were attracted by the variety of mystery cults which flourished during the first three centuries of the church. Merging a mystical spirituality with the fertile life cycles of nature, the mysteries offered eternal life and union with the divine through frenzied rites where, for example, the flesh of raw bulls was eaten or initiates were baptized in the dripping blood of sacrificed animals.[8] These cults had a great appeal to the less philosophically oriented who wanted something more exciting—an immediate, mystical, ecstatic experience of God.

Many people who had been initiated into mysteries responded positively to the preaching of the apostles. After all, here was a hope of salvation and eternal life based not on some esoteric inner knowledge, but on a historical person. At least five hundred people had seen Him after He was raised from the dead. Unlike the cults, they called people to a life of holiness and purity.[9] Paul hints that some of the Corinthians may have been involved in these cults prior to their conversion (see 1 Cor. 2:12).

Modern society alternates between the same two poles as the ancient world: despair and deep yearning for something more. Atheists may be right to criticize talk of life beyond the grave as "pie in the sky bye and bye," because often it is a vague aspiration, masking an overarching desire to be as comfortable here and now as possible. On the other hand, despair can often take the form of selfishness. When the myth of eternal progress disappears, as Christopher Lasch in *The True and Only Heaven:*

Progress and Its Critics argues that it has in Western culture, the result is hedonism. Volunteers become hard to find. Personal and corporate giving decline. Interest groups hound government for selfish ends, and no one considers public good, what life will be like after death, or what God must think of behavior.

But why think of the future if final destiny is what Bertrand Russell called the "vast death of the solar system"? Wouldn't it be better to focus on improving things here while we can? Hope for future blessing is simply a hindrance to usefulness now. So argue secularists who criticize believers in the Resurrection. However, traditionally, those with the clearest vision of the afterlife are the very ones who have worked hardest to improve the lot of others here on earth.[10] Without some vision of where life is headed, there is little reason to make present improvements. As Peter Kreeft says, "The pregnant woman who plans a live birth cares for her unborn baby; [but] the woman who plans for an abortion does not."[11]

Ancient Stoic pantheism has reappeared in our time in the dress of Eastern mysticism married to Western psychology: the New Age movement. In its obsession with life beyond the grave, it probes the paranormal for clues: ghosts, reincarnation, spirit guides, ESP, and a host of other phenomena surely prove that, since God is a part of the cosmic realm, humans are immortal. But if we listen carefully, the underlying despair can be heard behind all this gazing into a crystal ball. Scratch this neopantheism and you discover that it is not individual humans who are immortal but only the soul, that which is part of the Divine Being. The philosophy of reincarnation appears to say that humans return to this world again and again (though often under

---

Those with the clearest vision of the afterlife work hardest to improve the lot of others here on earth.

---

the forms of subhuman life). But what actually survives death in reincarnation is not human life at all; only that spark of divine life in us which is impersonal. Therefore, the ultimate "hope" of reincarnation is the obliteration of all that makes human life as we know it worth living.

The Resurrection of the Flesh

To counter efforts to restrict our redemption to some part of our humanity, the original words of the Apostles' Creed were "the resurrection of the flesh," not as in our modern versions, the "resurrection of the body." The use of that word "flesh" was striking: To Paul "flesh" was not only the body, but the total person in rebellion against God. Yet the word "flesh" was retained, for it made clear that it is our complete humanity that will one day be raised to newness of life.[12]

The final phrase of the Creed is "life everlasting."

This too has led to misunderstanding, since the emphasis in the New Testament is not on duration but on the quality of life beyond the grave. In fact, "eternal life," which is the preferred translation from the Greek, is simply life in union with God. Eternal life, being timeless, is therefore available to us here and now. "This *is* eternal life," said Jesus, "that they may know You, the only true God, and Jesus Christ whom You have sent" (John 17:3; italics mine). Many have easily mistaken eternal life for "everlasting life," especially because it is placed at the end of the Creed, giving rise to the jeers of skeptics that since it is sexless, without social or national distinction, and free of all cares, it must be incredibly boring.[13]

Unfinished Symphony

Is eternal life boring? I think of the experience of George Walker. As an ambulance sped him toward the hospital, George told a friend that a book he was writing about his struggle with cancer would have to be called his "Unfinished Symphony." The manuscript would be brief, but it would still be his testimony to hope in the resurrection of the body and eternal life. Here is a part of what he had to say:

For nearly fifty years, whenever I stopped to think about it, I had to admit to no satisfactory conclusion about the meaning of life and death. Sometimes death seemed to be a final destination, a place of no escape, a prison house. Sometimes it seemed a temporary stopover en route to becoming someone—or something—else. I remember wondering if the Hindus are right. Do we return to earth in a different form to live over and over again? Is death a matter of coming before the bar of cosmic justice, to receive a report card at the end of school? Do we graduate to the next class? Most often death has seemed like walking up to a heavy door. I never quite knew what was on the other side, but I could always sense great darkness.

George Walker was a businessman, a family man, and a lifelong churchman; but it took the dreaded word "cancer," uttered by his doctor, to bring him face-to-face with the reality that it was "all over." Or was it?

His first reaction was anger and bitterness.

I said things to God that I never thought I would find myself saying. I cursed him. I blasphemed. I raged against the God of heaven . . . Cajoling, demanding, pleading, bargaining, taunting—nothing worked. My temper tantrums gained me nothing. The awakening was rude and harsh.

He next searched for a medical miracle. There were long series of radiation treatments and operations. During this time he began to search the Scriptures, and his despair gradually began to diminish. He even found humor in his situation. For example, he found himself fantasizing over exotic foods even though he could barely digest a piece of toast!

I began to look pretty awful—my legs shriveled, my abdomen bulged. When I passed a mirror I could only think of my resemblance to some strange feathered wildlife, perhaps a migratory duck or a crow. Pathetic humor? Of course. But morbid humor? Never. The Lord gave us not only the ability to see through the situation, but also just enough humor to prove that his amazing grace is always available.

The testimony continues with an acceptance of grace, George's repentance, and the faith that came. Although his questions were not all answered, much of life was brought into focus for him.

The amazing thing about his grace was what *did* come into focus. How totally remarkable that the Lord should be using a vehicle like a fatal illness to give me an understanding of things I very probably might have missed altogether. How gracious of him to show me my utter dependence on him before it became too late! How wondrous his works! How majestic his revelation! To discover life's purpose is the purpose of life. And Jesus said, "I am the way, and the truth, and the life."

So now it remained for me to take the Lord's help so generously offered, and to prepare for what had to come. To pretend I have no apprehension would be to lie. But the fear is so much less than I might have expected.

George Walker's "Unfinished Symphony" concludes with a list of all the things that God had taught him through his illness. Among them were these things:

He has convinced me that death is not what is on the other side of a door, but only the journey through the doorway itself.

He has placed considerations of materialism into proper perspective once and for all.

He has brought his Holy Spirit, the great comforter, to bear in a most sure and positive way.

He has made the word "transitory" meaningful rather than futile, as it might have become.

He has assured us that the future is not a thing to be feared, for he holds it in his hand.

He has kept his promise to be with us—even to the end.

He has stabilized the pace of fast-beating hearts, brought childlike joys back to ego-centered adult minds.

He has reestablished heaven as a place where those who follow him will have a table prepared for them.

He has . . .[14]

George Walker was too weak to write anymore and died shortly afterward.

Three Images

There are three biblical images which encapsulate the wonderful benefits and joys which we may anticipate in the life to come. They also highlight the challenge of the Christian hope.

Our most basic captivity is neither economic, nor psychological, nor metaphysical; it is moral.

Victory

Christ's resurrection is the ultimate victory over the powers of death and destruction (see 1 Cor. 15:55). Elisabeth Kübler-Ross writes that it makes no difference how the meaning of death is interpreted. All that matters is that you find peace, comfort, and acceptance about your own death.[15] But we are not able to domesticate death as if it were a wild animal that needs only a tamer's touch. Death is an affront and an outrage to life.[16] For God to reign supreme over His creation, death must be overcome.

Jesus lives: thy terrors now
Can, O death, no more appal us;
Jesus lives: by this we know

Thou, O grave, canst not enthral us.
Alleluia!

Jesus lives: to Him the throne
Over all the world is given:
May we go where He is gone,
Rest and reign with Him in heaven.
Alleluia![17]

Liberty

Contrary to modern thought, our most basic captivity is neither economic, nor psychological, nor metaphysical; it is moral. Sin's strong web has succeeded in tying us in knots, so that we are not free to love, laugh, praise God, or fulfill our real destiny. We are in bondage to failure and the fear of more failure. Never are we more bound than when we try to break out of social convention and assert our independence. At that point precisely, we are most at the mercy of our appetites.

But God has a dream that unfolds only to the eyes of faith. With every experience of futility we trace creation's longing for the liberation that will come when the stuff of our physical lives is brought back into full, complete harmony with the Spirit of God, and the human family is reconnected with its loving Father (see Rom. 8:19–23).

Rest

In our world we are tempted to think that action validates itself. We do not ask why or wherefore but simply keep moving. People imagine that by sheer activity they can escape the haunting question:

who am I? But to this madness God says: rest! God gives the Sabbath to remind us that "there remains . . . a rest for the people of God" (Heb. 4:9). Augustine saw the Sabbath as an integral part of the restoration of our true humanity. He wrote: "On the seventh day we shall be ourselves."[18]

Simply put, activity and effort are not the final word. After the storm there is rest, and after the final struggle with death, there is the "peace of God, which surpasses all understanding" (Phil. 4:7).

> O Lord, support us all the day long of this troublous life, until the shadows lengthen and the evening comes, the busy world is hushed, the fever of life is over, and our work is done. Then, Lord, in thy mercy, grant us a safe lodging, a holy rest, and peace at the last; through Jesus Christ our Lord.[19]

Victory, liberation, peace. Far from rendering the struggle with decay, sin, and meaningless activity unnecessary, the sure and certain hope of the Resurrection justifies and motivates that struggle. Yet at the same time, we are freed from the idolatry of worldliness. As Malcolm Muggeridge once said, "The only ultimate disaster that can befall us is to feel ourselves at home here on earth."

Questions for Discussion

1. Where do you see the denial of death in modern society?

2. Why is J. B. Priestley's description of himself as a "nullifidian" an oxymoron?

3. Why does a belief in the immortality of the soul lead
   to the conclusion that "matter doesn't matter"?

4. How is moral transformation *now* related to a belief in
   the ultimate resurrection of the body?

5. How do you understand Augustine's statement, "On the
   seventh day we shall be ourselves"?

NOTES

1. Encountering Truth in a Relativistic Age

1. Robert N. Bellah, *Habits of the Heart* (New York: Harper & Row, 1985), 155–162, 277.

2. "Freedom of Thought, a Principle in Peril?", *Yale Alumni Magazine,* October 1989; "A Purposeful Perplexity," *Yale Alumni Magazine,* October 1988.

3. For an analysis and critique of these and other ideologies competing with the Christian claim see my *Disarming the Secular Gods* (Downers Grove: InterVarsity Press, 1989).

4. Some doctrinal enthusiasts will take issue here. They fear that to desire "unity" before we know whether we have any "truth" to be united about sinks the starting point of our discussion into the murky ground of pragmatism rather than placing it on the firm foundation of revelation. I urge them to consider: The question about community must be asked because truth never exists in

the abstract. Truth is communal, expressing the deepest beliefs of a group of people who claim to see the world similarly. Just as other sacred books are hardly understandable except in the framework of those communities in which they are revered, so the Bible is neither understandable nor, for that matter, credible apart from the context of faith and obedience in which Christians have lived and died through the centuries.

5. Second Baptist Church, Houston, Texas.

6. Richard N. Longnecker, in *New Testament Social Ethics for Today,* argues that political reasons, evangelistic priorities, and a primary concern for the ethical quality of family relationships (where slaves were often trusted members of the household) caused Paul not to develop the full implications of his insight that "in Christ" there is neither slave nor free. However, the fact that masters and slaves could be addressed as equals before God undercut the institution of slavery and led to its eventual demise. (Grand Rapids: William B. Eerdmans, 1984), 48–69.

7. Michael Green, *Evangelism in the Early Church* (Grand Rapids: William B. Eerdmans, 1970), 207–223.

8. Toynbee's modern equivalents are those theologians like John Hick and even Hans Kung who insist that in order for interfaith dialogue to flourish, all participants must subject their truth claims to the relativizing standards of modernity. But as Mark Heim points out, this is to force all religions to accept the hegemony of Western thought—something many, if not most, are quite unwilling to do. See S. Mark Heim, "Pluralism and the

Otherness of World Religions," *First Things,* August/September 1992, 29–35.

9. For a helpful discussion of the meaning of tolerance see Harold A. Netland, *Dissonant Voices: Religious Pluralism and the Question Of Truth* (Grand Rapids: William B. Eerdmans, 1991), 301–314. Toynbee's plea is found in Arnold Toynbee, *Christianity Among the Religions of the World* (New York: Charles Scribner's Sons, 1957), 95f.

10. John Naisbitt and Patricia Aburdene, *Megatrends 2000* (New York: Avon Books, 1990), 290ff. Alvin Toffler, *Power Shift* (New York: Bantam Books, 1990), 456–458.

11. "A Time to Seek," *Newsweek,* 17 December 1990, 50–56.

12. Joy Davidman, *Smoke on the Mountain, The Ten Commandments in Terms of Today* (London: Hodder & Stoughton, 1955), 36.

13. "... Tillich and Bultmann, two premier 'modern' theologians, were not so modern. They both bought into the notion, conventional wisdom at least since Schleiermacher (no, since Constantine), that the challenge of Christianity was primarily an intellectual one involving the clash of two different systems of belief: how to make old Christianity credible to the new modern world. Which explains why Karl Barth was much more 'new' than Tillich. Tillich still thought that the theological challenge involved the creation of a new and better-adapted systematic theology. Barth knew that the theological problem was the creation of a new and better church. Tillich hoped that, by the time one had finished his *Sys-*

tematic Theology, one would think about things differently. Barth hoped that, by the time one had plodded through his *Church Dogmatics,* one would *be* different." Stanley Hauerwas and William H. Willimon, *Resident Aliens* (Nashville: Abingdon Press, 1990), 23–24.

14. At the Seventh World Council of Churches in Canberra, Australia, Feb. 1991, keynote speaker Prof. Chung Kyung-Hyung of Korea invoked ancestor spirits and said that the best "image of the Holy Spirit comes from the image of *Kwan In* . . . [who] is venerated as goddess of compassion and wisdom in East Asian women's popular religion." Tourists can buy tea mugs, T-shirts, and home altar decorations honoring *Kwan In* in most oriental bazaars. Lawrence E. Adams, "The WCC at Canberra: Which Spirit?", *First Things* (14 June/July 1991), 30.

15. In his stimulating study of American religion, Jewish agnostic Harold Bloom claims that the spirit which undergirds most religions which trace their origins to American soil (Adventists, Jehovah's Witnesses, Christian Scientists, Mormons, New Agers—but also, surprisingly, such orthodox stalwarts as Pentecostals and Southern Baptists) is not that of historic biblical or creedal Christianity but of Gnosticism. His often humorous critique turns into blistering polemic as he repeatedly anathematizes conservatives within the Southern Baptist Convention as "Know-Nothing Fundamentalists"—a phrase that reveals his own prejudice to be very close to the Gnosticism he criticizes. Harold Bloom, *The American Religion: The Emergence of the Post Christian Nation* (New York: Simon and Schuster, 1992).

16. References are made throughout the endnotes to a number of works based on the Apostles' Creed.

17. Yves Congar, *I Believe in the Holy Spirit,* vol. II (New York: The Seabury Press, 1983), 115.

18. Adapted from J. Manning Potts, ed., *Prayers of the Early Church* (Nashville: The Upper Room, 1953), 52.

2. An Eternal Contradiction?

1. Barbara Withers, ed., *An Inclusive Language Lectionary* (Atlanta, Philadelphia, New York: John Knox, Westminster, Pilgrim, 1991).

2. Donald G. Bloesch, *The Battle for the Trinity, The Debate Over Inclusive God Language* (Ann Arbor: Servant Publications, 1985), 33, 47.

3. Rosemary Ruether, *Sexism and God-Talk* (Boston: Beacon Press, 1983), 38–41.

4. Bloesch, *Battle for the Trinity*, 40.

5. Harry Blamires, *The Christian Mind* (Ann Arbor: Servant Books, 1978), 137.

6. Ibid., 138.

7. Robert Bly, *Iron John* (Reading: Adison-Wesley Publishing Co. Inc., 1990), 122.

8. After receiving letters of protest, the bishop recalled the offending liturgies and suggested trinitarian ones in their place.

9. "The divine nature is infinite, exceeding the scope of all human concepts, and is capable of being experienced both as personal Lord and as nonpersonal ground or depth of being." John Hick in *God Has Many Names* (Philadelphia: Westminster, 1982), 38. For a rebuttal to Hick's thesis, see Harold A. Netland, *Dissonant Voices: Religious Pluralism and the Question of Truth* (Grand Rapids: William B. Eerdmans, 1991), 196–233.

10. Jan Milic Lochman, *The Faith We Confess, An Ecumenical Dogmatics,* trans. David Lewis (Philadelphia: Fortress, 1984), 53.

11. James Stalker, *The Ethic of Jesus,* quoted in Herbert Lockyer, *Everything Jesus Taught,* vol. 1 (New York: Harper & Row, 1976), 66.

12. Peter Kreeft, *Fundamentals of Christian Theology* (San Francisco: Ignatius Press, 1988), 124.

13. Bloesch, *Battle For The Trinity,* 37–38.

3. Man Without Parallel

1. J. S. Whale, *Christian Doctrine* (Cambridge: The University Press, 1950), 108.

2. Malcolm Muggeridge, *Confessions of a Twentieth Century Pilgrim* (San Francisco: Harper & Row, 1988), 131, 140.

3. Edna Sarah Beardsley, *The Word, A Philosophy of Words* (San Francisco, 1958), 32–33.

4. Walter Trobish, *The Misunderstood Male* (Downers Grove: InterVarsity Press, 1983), 62.

5. "Trust in any sort of gods has become frail and super-fluous. These are the gods set up, honoured and wor-shipped by men in ancient and recent times: The authorities on whom man relies . . . Faith delivers us from trust in such gods, and therefore also fear of them . . ." Karl Barth, *Dogmatics in Outline,* trans. G. T. Thomson (London: SCM Press, 1958), 19.

6. F. F. Bruce, *The Spreading Flame* (London: The Pater-noster Press, 1958), 245.

7. J. N. D. Anderson, *The Mystery of the Incarnation* (Sevenoaks: Hodder & Stoughton, Ltd., 1978), 30.

8. J. V. Langmead Casserley, *Apologetics and Evange-lism* (Philadelphia: The Westminster Press, 1962), 112.

9. John Stott, *Issues Facing Christians Today* (Basing-stoke, Marshall Morgan & Scott, 1984), 19.

10. Anderson, *Mystery of the Incarnation,* 56.

11. For a discussion of the modern "isms" that vie with historic Christianity see my *Disarming the Secular Gods* (Downers Grove: InterVarsity Press, 1989). A discussion of miracles appears on pp. 145–147.

12. See Matt. 11:27; 21:37; 24:36; Mark 1:1; Luke 1:32; John 1:1; 8:58; Acts 2:36; 1 Cor. 8:6; Phil. 2:6–11; Col. 1:15–17, 19; Heb. 1:3. The late Bishop Stephen Neill, who was well acquainted with other religions, wrote: "[Christian faith]

maintains that in Jesus the one thing that needed to happen has happened in such a way that it need never happen again in the same way. The universe has been reconciled to its God. Through the perfect obedience of one man a new and permanent relationship has been established between God and the whole human race. The bridge has been built. There is room on it for all the needed traffic in both directions, from God to man and from man to God. Why look for any other?" Stephen Neill, *Crises of Belief* (London: Hodder & Stoughton, 1984), 31. First printed as *Christian Faith And Other Faiths* (London: Oxford University Press, 1961).

13. While this was a special contribution of Origen, J. N. D. Kelly points out that the preexistence of Christ was an idea solidly grasped by the Apostolic Fathers (Clement of Rome, Ignatius, Hermas) of the second century. J. N. D. Kelly, *Early Christian Doctrines* (London: Adam and Charles Black, 1958), 90–94.

14. Arians, following Arius (c. 250–336), argued that Jesus was "of like substance" with the Father (Gk., *homoiousios*). Athanasius (c. 296–373) countered that Jesus was "of the same substance" as the Father (Gk., *homoousios*). Athanasius carried the day, and the latter phrase has passed into the Nicene Creed as the standard statement of Christian orthodoxy. For a full discussion of modern challenges to the classical statement of the full divinity of Jesus, see Donald G. Bloesch, *Essentials of Evangelical Theology,* vol. 1 (New York: Harper & Row, 1978), 120–142.

15. A contemporary example of the confusion might be the following: "Every statement about God is inevitably

inadequate, expressing one among many possible 'projections' of his reality; and it may be that manifold ways of expression are the only way in which we can dimly perceive the depth of riches beyond. So, if we say that 'God is disclosed in the man Jesus,' we may all perceive different facets, so that a multiplicity of christologies is inevitable by the very nature of our subject. To recognize this can only help to enrich and deepen our theology." Frances Young, "A Cloud of Witnesses" in John Hick, ed., *The Myth of God Incarnate* (Philadelphia: The Westminster Press, 1977), 40.

16. Quoted in Donald Bloesch, *Essentials of Evangelical Theology,* vol. 1 (New York, Harper & Row, 1978), 120.

17. Hugh Schonfield, *Those Incredible Christians* (New York: Bantam, 1969), 237–239.

18. James M. Houston, ed., *The Mind on Fire: An Anthology of the Writings of Blaise Pascal* (Portland: Multnomah Press, 1989), 149f.

19. Sören Kierkegaard, *Training in Christianity* (Princeton: The University Press, 1957), 44.

4. Second Adam to the Rescue

1. On September 22, 1891, Pope Leo XIII's encyclical "Octobri Mense" called Mary "mediatrix to the Mediator"; that is, by being the willing receptacle of God's grace we, through her, receive God's grace, and the work of redemption is thereby made effective for us. She is, therefore, co-redeemer. Because of the emphasis on the Virgin

Mary, Muslims usually think that the Christian doctrine of the Trinity is the Father, the Son, and the Virgin Mary. See Helmut Thielicke, *The Evangelical Faith,* vol. 3 (Grand Rapids: William B. Eerdmans, 1982), 49–53.

2. See discussion on Docetism in chapter 3.

3. William Barclay, *The Plain Man Looks at the Apostles' Creed* (London: Collins/Fontana, 1967), 81.

4. Benjamin B. Warfield, *Biblical Foundations* (London: Tyndale Press, 1958), 126.

5. W. H. Griffith Thomas, *The Principles of Theology* (London: Church Book Room Press, 1956), 49.

6. Justin Martyr in A.D. 150 writes: "Our Teacher Jesus Christ, who is the first-begotten of God the Father, was not born as a result of sexual relations . . . the power of God descending upon the virgin overshadowed her, and caused her, while still a virgin, to conceive. For by God's power He was conceived by a virgin." *Apology* 1:21–33. Interestingly, renowned conservative theologian Leon Morris writes a book titled *The Lord from Heaven* on the divinity and humanity of Jesus in which the virgin birth is barely mentioned. (London: InterVarsity Fellowship, 1958).

7. C. S. Lewis, *Miracles, A Preliminary Study* (London: Geoffrey Bles, 1957), 72, 73. For an extensive discussion of miracles and modern science, read Charles E. Hummel, *The Galileo Connection* (Downers Grove: InterVarsity Press, 1986), 188–197.

8. "It may be conceded that there is in the modern world a certain type of consciousness that has difficulties with the supernatural . . . We may say that contemporary consciousness is such and such; we are left with the question of whether we will assent to it. We may agree, say, that contemporary consciousness is incapable of conceiving either angels or demons. We are still left with the question of whether, possibly, both angels and demons go on existing despite this incapacity of our contemporaries to conceive of them." Peter L. Berger, *A Rumor of Angels* (Garden City: Doubleday & Co., Inc., 1969), 52–53.

9. "Anyone who claims to be able personally to [believe in the world of spirits and of miracles as we find it set forth in the New Testament] must recognize that, if he presents this as the attitude which is required of Christian believers, he is making Christian preaching incomprehensible and impossible of acceptance in the modern world." Rudolf Bultmann, quoted by Giovanni Meigge, *Gospel and Myth in the Thought of Rudolf Bultmann* (Richmond: John Knox, 1960), 8.

10. Emil Brunner, *The Mediator,* trans. O. Wyon (London: Lutterworth Press, 1934), 322–327.

11. Lewis, *Miracles,* 57.

12. Donald Bloesch, *Essentials of Evangelical Theology,* vol. 1 (New York: Harper & Row, 1978), 131.

13. Jan Milic Lochman, *The Faith We Confess, An Ecumenical Dogmatics,* trans. David Lewis (Philadelphia: Fortress, 1984), 107.

14. Karl Barth, *Dogmatics in Outline,* trans. G. T. Tomson (London: SCM Press, 1949), 100.

15. John Irving, *A Prayer for Owen Meany* (Toronto: Ballantine Books, 1989), 540–541.

16. Lochman, *The Faith We Confess,* 112. "[Barth's] view is open to various objections. In addition to its sexist overtones, it appears to teach the total depravity of all males! But Barth is not without justice in applying the doctrine of the virgin birth to the realm of grace." Sinclair B. Ferguson, David F. Wright, J. I. Packer, eds. *New Dictionary of Theology* (Downers Grove: InterVarsity Press, 1988), 710.

17. John Henry Newman, 1865, *Anglican Hymn Book* (London: Vine, 1965), 160.

5. Dancing with the Devil on Your Back

1. "Whatever their differences . . . Joseph Butler, Fredrich Schleiermacher, Albert Ritschl, Emil Brunner, Rudolph Bultmann, Carl Rahner, Wolfhart Pannenberg and Jurgen Moltmann [and many others] agreed . . . that the religious meaningfulness of the claim [that Jesus Christ is the Redeemer] . . . must be perspicuous through its relation to other accounts of general human experience." Hans W. Frei, *The Eclipse of Biblical Narrative* (New Haven: Yale, 1974), 128.

2. "If we speak only of Christ suffering and dying, we overlook the initiative of the Father. If we speak only of God suffering and dying, we overlook the mediation of

the Son. The New Testament authors never attribute the atonement either to Christ in such a way as to disassociate him from the Father, or to God in such a way as to dispense with Christ, but rather to God and Christ." John Stott, *The Cross of Christ* (Downers Grove: InterVarsity Press, 1986), 156.

3. C. S. Lewis, *Miracles, A Preliminary Study* (London: Geoffrey Bles, 1957), 136.

4. John A. T. Robinson, *Honest To God* (London: SCM Press, 1963), 45–63.

5. In the *Honest To God Debate,* Leonard Griffiths, then Minister of the City Temple in London, rejoined: "To be sure, Tillich, Bultmann and Bonhoeffer might replace the God 'out there' with a God 'in here,' but they are not the only prophets of Christianity in our age. Alongside them stand other theological giants, men like Karl Barth, Reinhold Niebuhr and Emil Brunner, who hold very firmly to the traditional image of a God separate and distinct from the world which he has made . . . This has nothing to do with the dimensions of outer space; it is simply a means of saying what the Bible repeatedly says and what human experience proves, namely, that *God is not man,* that he stands over against man, creating him, providing for him, judging him and redeeming him. What really matters in this view is not what the Bishop thinks about God, but what God thinks of the Bishop." (Philadelphia: The Westminster Press, 1963), 101–102.

6. "The . . . reason why it is misleading to say that 'God died' is that 'God' in the New Testament frequently means 'the Father' (e.g., 'God sent his Son'), and the per-

son who died on the cross was not the Father but the Son." Stott, *The Cross of Christ,* 155. It is difficult, however, to see how one can avoid saying that God "tasted death" in the light of a fully biblical christology, and a passage such as Heb. 2:9.

7. See also Psalm 69:1–3, and 14–17 where the depths, the flood, the mire all are symbols not only of imminent death, but also of profound separation from God.

8. G. W. Target, *We, The Crucifiers* (London: Hodder and Stoughton, Ltd., 1964), 138–139, 141; quoted in Mary McDermott Shideler, *A Creed for a Christian Skeptic* (Grand Rapids: William B. Eerdmans, 1968), 107–108.

9. Edward Shillito, "Jesus of the Scars," quoted by William Temple, *Readings in St. John's Gospel,* 2 vols. (New York: Macmillan, 1940), 384–385.

10. Douglas Webster, *In Debt to Christ* (London: Highway Press, 1957), 46 quoted in Stott, *The Cross of Christ,* 78.

11. Stott, *The Cross of Christ,* 149.

12. P. T. Forsythe, *Cruciality of the Cross* (London: Hodder and Stoughton, 1909), 205–206.

13. "Good Friday" (also titled "Substitution") by Peter Rodgers. Used by permission.

14. Luther and Calvin differed on the meaning of the descent into hell. Building on the standard texts, Job 38:17; Ps. 68:18–22; Matt. 12:38–41; Acts 2:22–32; Rom. 10:7; Eph. 4:7–10; 1 Peter 3:18–20; 4:6, Luther argued that

Christ's descent was a positive mission to bring deliverance to saints of the old covenant, while Calvin argued that it was part of Christ's experience of dereliction. I have argued for the latter, following Anselm's famous expression: "You have not yet considered the full weight of sin." See Jan Milic Lochman, *The Faith We Confess, An Ecumenical Dogmatics,* trans., David Lewis (Philadelphia: Fortress, 1984), 144–145.

6. Sign of the Chrysalis

1. Michael Green, *The Empty Cross of Jesus* (Downers Grove: InterVarsity Press, 1984), 95.

2. "Agamemnon sacrificed his daughter Iphigenia to avert the wrath of Artemis and secure the success of the Trojan War." Green points out that "the theme [of sacrifice] plays a prominent role in no less than five of Euripides' plays *(Alcestis, Hecuba, Heraclidae, Phoenissae,* and *Supplices)*." Ibid., 139.

3. Ibid., 145.

4. Gilbert Murray, *Five Stages of Greek Religion* (Garden City: Doubleday, 1951), 144.

5. Cecil Frances Alexander, 1846, *The Book of Common Praise* (Toronto: Anglican Book Centre, 1929), 157.

6. Abraham J. Heschel, *The Prophets* vol. I (New York: Harper Colophon Books, 1962), 19.

7. *Epistles* X.96. For a full discussion of the correspondence between Pliny and Trajan, see F. F. Bruce, *New Testament History* (Garden City: Doubleday, 1972), 422–425.

8. Feodor Dostoyevsky, *The Brothers Karamazov,* vol. 1 (Middlesex: Penguin, 1958), 301.

9. A. Toynbee, *A Study of History* vol. I (New York: Oxford University Press, 1946), 493–494.

10. Dietrich Bonhoeffer, *Letters and Papers from Prison* (New York: Macmillan, 1953), 154, 14.

11. G. W. H. Lampe and D. M. MacKinnon, *The Resurrection* (Philadelphia: The Westminster Press, 1966), 97.

12. Joseph Klausner, *Jesus of Nazareth,* quoted by Green, *The Empty Cross of Jesus,* 102. See 92–103 for a fuller summary of evidence on the empty tomb.

13. Nicholas Woltersdorff, *Lament for a Son* (Grand Rapids: William B. Eerdmans, 1987), 92.

14. John Updike, *Telephone Poles and Other Poems.* (New York: Knopf, 1961), 72–73. Reprinted by permission of Alfred A. Knopf, Inc.

7. Humanity on Trial

1. C. S. Lewis, *God in the Dock, Essays on Theology and Ethics* (Grand Rapids: William B. Eerdmans, 1970), 288.

2. From *After the Fall* by Arthur Miller. Copyright © 1964 by Arthur Miller. Used by permission of Viking Penguin, a division of Penguin Books USA Inc.

3. William Barrett, *Irrational Man, A Study in Existential Philosophy* (Garden City: Doubleday/Anchor, 1962), 247. Paul Johnson points out that such a low evaluation of the self did not prevent Sartre and other Existentialists from advocating action, especially radical action, when they felt the cause warranted it. Sartre was in fact fascinated with violence throughout his life, and his pupil, Franz Fanon, published in 1961 "the most influential of all terrorist handbooks *(The Damned of the Earth)*." *Modern Times, The World From The Twenties to the Eighties* (New York: Harper Colophon Books, 1983), 687.

4. *Waiting for Godot* touched a raw nerve in post-World War II European society; it ran for more than sixteen months to packed houses in the capitals of Europe.

5. Alan Astro, *Understanding Samuel Beckett* (Columbia: University of South Carolina Press, 1990), 120. Beckett commented in an interview: "I am interested in the shape of ideas even if I do not believe in them. There is a wonderful sentence in Augustine . . . 'Do not despair; one of the thieves was saved. Do not presume; one of the thieves was damned.' That sentence has a wonderful shape. It is the shape that matters." See "Love, Chess and Death," *Twentieth Century* 164 (December 1958), 537.

6. A brief survey of verses includes 1 Thess. 5:2; Phil. 1:6; 1 Tim. 6:14; Col. 3:4; Eph. 4:30; Titus 2:12–13; James 5:8; 1 Peter 1:5; 4:7; 2 Peter 3:10; Acts 1:11; 3:19–21; 10:42; 17:31; John 5:26–29; 6:39; 14:3; 16:16–22.

7. William Barclay, *New Testament Words* (London: SCM Press, 1964), 223.

8. For a full summary of this view see William Barclay, *The Plain Man Looks at the Apostles' Creed* (London: Collins, 1967), 199–239.

9. G. W. H. Lampe, "The Atonement: Law and Love", in Alec Vidler, *Soundings, Essays Concerning Christian Understanding* (Cambridge: The University Press, 1964), 188–189.

10. David L. Edwards, *Essentials, A Liberal-Evangelical Dialogue* (London: Hodder & Stoughton, 1988), 336.

11. A brief survey of references to hell and judgment includes Matt. 5:29, 30; 7:13; 8:12; 22:13; 25:30, 46; Mark 3:29; 9:43, 44; Luke 16:26; John 3:16, cf. 2 Peter 3:9; Heb. 3:11; 10:31.

12. See N. T. Wright, "Universalism," in Sinclair B. Ferguson, David F. Wright, J. I. Packer, eds., *New Dictionary of Theology* (Downers Grove: InterVarsity Press, 1988), 703.

13. Jonathan Edwards's famous sermon "Sinners in the hands of an angry God," in which he said that "the God that holds you over the pit of hell much in the same manner as one holds a spider or some loathesome insect over the fire, abhors you and is dreadfully provoked," is a sermon which Richard Lovelace says "New England has never forgotten, and never forgiven!"

14. Edwards, *Essentials,* 318. Carl F. H. Henry argues that the Greek word *aionios* (eternal) is used of both heaven and hell to denote "endless consequences." Leon Morris, while taking the image of "fire" as only one biblical image of hell, believes that the fate of the wicked must not be seen as anything less permanent than that of believers. However, in reply, it could be argued that destruction is just as permanent as endless torture. See Phil. 3:19. Carl F. H. Henry, *God, Revelation and Authority,* Part Two (Waco: Word Books, 1983), 510; Leon Morris, "Hell, the Dreadful Harvest," *Christianity Today,* 27 May 1991, 36.

15. T. F. Torrance, *The School of Faith: The Catechisms of the Reformed Church* (London: J. Clarke & Co., 1959), 78, as Jan Milic Lochman quoted in *An Ecumenical Dogmatics, The Faith We Confess,* trans. David Lewis (Philadelphia: Fortress, 1984), 172–173.

16. Leon Morris, *The Apostolic Preaching of the Cross* (London: Tyndale Press, 1960), 158.

17. Mary McDermott Shideler, *A Creed for a Christian Skeptic* (Grand Rapids: William B. Eerdmans, 1968), 130.

8. Go-Between God

1. Analogies that convey the true nature of the Trinity are difficult to find. The three persons are one "substance," as traditional orthodoxy has put it. Muslims and Jews often accuse Christians of tritheism, the belief that there is not one God, but three. However, "[Tritheism only arises] if the persons of the Trinity are regarded as substantial beings in their own right, sharing a common

divinity only in the sense that people share a common humanity." G. L. Bray, "Tritheism," in Sinclair B. Ferguson, David F. Wright, J. I. Packer, eds., *New Dictionary of Theology* (Downers Grove: InterVarsity Press, 1988), 694.

2. Robert N. Bellah, *Habits of the Heart* (New York: Harper & Row, 1985), 142–163.

3. Reginald W. Bibby, *Mosaic Madness: The Poverty and Potential of Life in Canada* (Toronto: Stoddart, 1990), 71.

4. Paul was given the clearest vision of this understanding of the church as diversity within unity. Eventually all the other apostles joined him, but not without some qualms of conscience. See Acts 10:34–43; 15:1–29; Gal. 2:11–21; 3:28.

5. William Barclay, *New Testament Words* (London: SCM Press Ltd., 1964), 173.

6. ". . . recall Lessing's view of history. Humanity as a child is taught by the event and word of revelation until its own spirit takes over the leadership and appropriates by the autonomous insight of reason the truth that has hitherto been authoritatively imparted to it. In this eschatological age of fulfillment the Spirit of God seems as it were to be identical with the human spirit, just as we see the absolute spirit and the inner spring merging according to Hegel's teaching." Helmut Thielicke, *The Evangelical Faith,* vol. 3 (Grand Rapids: William B. Eerdmans, 1982), 24.

7. George Vandervelde, ed., *The Holy Spirit, Renewing and Empowering Presence* (Winfield: Wood Lake Books, 1989), 23.

8. William Temple, *Christian Faith and Life* (London: SCM Press, Ltd., 1931), 94, 96, 101, my paraphrase.

9. "The Spirit's distinct personhood can, and according to the NT should, be read into the OT, but cannot be read out of it." J. I. Packer, *New Dictionary of Theology* (Downers Grove: InterVarsity Press, 1988), 316.

10. "[Pentecostals] are wrong in making Pentecost only and primarily an experience of empowering. On the contrary, the Baptism in the Spirit, as always, is primarily initiatory, and only secondarily an empowering. The fact is that the phrase 'baptism in Spirit' is never directly associated with the promise of power, but is always associated with entry into the messianic age or the Body of Christ." James D. G. Dunn, *Baptism in the Holy Spirit* (Naperville: Alec R. Allenson, Inc., 1970), 54.

11. Thielicke, *The Evangelical Faith,* 75.

12. Spoken at the Diocese of Toronto's Conference on Renewal, August, 1987.

13. Karl Barth, *Dogmatics in Outline* (New York: Harper & Row, 1959), 139.

14. "Speaking in tongues in modern Pentecostalism may be completely inarticulate utterance (though more than baby-talk) but it may also be speaking in a foreign language which observes grammatical rules and syntax." Thielicke, 81, referring to Dennis Bennett's book *Nine O'Clock in the Morning,* 21ff. However, despite occasional testimonies that people have claimed to have heard a tongue in a language that they have known, the language

quality of *glossolalia* has been challenged by Toronto linguist William Samarin whose extensive study *Tongues of Men and Angels* concluded that it did not observe grammatical rules and syntax (New York: Macmillan, 1972).

15. For a taste of the book which spoke most powerfully to me: "The Pentecostal evidence [of tongues] is not simply a harmless idiosyncrasy which can be smiled upon in its naivete and passed by . . . it bears the marks of the demand in the early church for circumcision." "In fact the Penetecostal progression—beyond the Lord to the Spirit—is prevented . . . by the definition of the Spirit's essential work as the confession of Jesus . . . (and) by proceeding from the Spirit to the Lord, which is the evangelical progression." In Corinth the "superlative apostles [claimed] that Paul made Christians in name, they made Christians in Spirit; Paul accented a crucified Messiah who gave grace, they brought a glorified Messiah who gave power; Paul brought the Spirit, but they brought him fully; Paul, in other words, brought something of the gospel, but they brought the full gospel." "Power, the divine answer told Paul, comes not through overcoming weakness but through bearing it. Some weaknesses are apparently never to be overcome, they are to be used." Frederick Dale Bruner, *A Theology of the Holy Spirit* (Grand Rapids: William B. Eerdmans, 1970), 282, 289, 309, 313.

9. Defying the Gates of Hell

1. "Liberal theology had spent decades reassuring us that we did not have to take the Jewishness of Jesus seriously. The particulars of this faith, the limiting, historically contingent, narrative specifics of the faith, such

as the Jewishness of Jesus or his messianic eschatology, were impediments for the credibility of modern people and could therefore be removed so that we could get down to the real substance of Christianity. Jesus was not *really* a Jew, he was the pinnacle of the brightest and best in humanity, the teacher of noble ideals, civilization's very best. It was a short step from the liberal Christ-the-highest-in-humanity to the Nazi Superman." Stanley Hauerwas and William H. Willimon, *Resident Aliens* (Nashville: Abingdon Press, 1989), 25.

2. The English word "church" is derived from the Greek *kuriakos* which means "belonging to the Lord."

3. In a book titled *On The Thirty-Nine Articles, A Conversation With Tudor Christianity,* Oliver O'Donovan, Regius Professor of Moral Theology at Oxford, criticizes his own communion for adding additional "marks" of the true church: "The Anglican church has itself been guilty of devising exclusive criteria for churchliness, which have allowed it to discount bodies which did not meet its standards. The Lambeth Quadrilateral of 1888 stipulated, as a condition of intercommunion with any church body, that it must have the Bible, the Creeds, the Sacraments and—the 'historic episcopate,' a bullying and unfriendly gesture to the non-episcopal churches which history, and Anglican second thoughts, have happily overtaken." (Exeter: The Paternoster Press, 1986), 95. See a further discussion on episcopacy and the marks of the church in my *A Church to Believe In* (Lexington: Bristol, 1994).

4. A distinction can be made between the hiddenness of the kingdom and the visibility of the church: "The kingdom of Christ is presently hidden in the structures of

history, but its revelation and consummation are still ahead of us in the absolute future of God." Donald G. Bloesch, *Essentials of Evangelical Theology,* vol. 2 (New York: Harper & Row, 1979), 151. Criticizing the Reformers for their lack of a clear theology of the church, O'Donovan tries to steer a middle ground between the visible/invisible antithesis favored by Luther and Calvin. He finds that in the concept of the church catholic: "To speak of the work of Christ it is necessary to speak of its result: a restored humanity, with Christ as its head, living in the light of God's presence. The catholic church is as much of that restored humanity as we have so far been given to see, a community in which the Holy Spirit dwells, expectantly anticipating the revealing of God's kingdom. Anyone who believes in Christ in response to the apostles' testimony and has the Holy Spirit dwelling within him is *ipso facto* part of the catholic church." O'Donovan, *On The Thirty-Nine Articles,* 93.

5. "We are heirs of the Christendom experiment. We who belong to the Western world live in societies that have been shaped by more than a thousand years during which the barbarous and savage tribes of Europe were brought, slowly and with many setbacks, into a community conceived as the *corpus Christianum,* a single society in which the whole of public and private life was to be controlled by the Christian revelation. The *corpus Christianum* is no more, and we cannot go back to it." Lesslie Newbigin, *Foolishness to the Greeks, The Gospel and Western Culture* (Grand Rapids: William B. Eerdmans, 1986), 101.

6. Hauerwas and Willimon, *Resident Aliens,* 42.

7. Os Guinness, in "Mission in the Face of Modernity," a series of lectures given at the Lausanne II Congress on World Evangelization in Manila, 1989, writes, "Christendom's ultimate worldling today is not the Christian liberal but the Christian conservative. The contemporary Church's prototypical charlatan is not the medieval priest but the modern evangelist. The Tetzels of history and the Elmer Gantrys of fiction pale beside the real life examples of evangelical and evangelistic worldliness in our own time."

8. "The Spirit is the prosecutor who brings the fundamental axioms of a culture under judgment (John 15:18–27)." Newbigin, *Foolishness to the Greeks,* 53. Striking a balance, Os Guinness says: "The Protagonist principle and the Antagonist principle must never be separated... Without the former, the latter would create a we/they division which is Manichean and not biblical. The Protagonist principle means there must be no hatred of the world or false asceticism with us. Yes, the world is passing away, and we are passing through the world. But the responsible realism of that bifocal vision should shape our perspective. Holding these two truths together, we are to be, in Peter Berger's memorable phrase, 'against the world for the world.'" "Mission in the Face of Modernity."

9. In a book designed to give a theological justification for the United Church of Canada's 1988 decision to admit practicing homosexuals to ordination, editor Pamela Dickey Young writes: "The community of faith remains a vehicle for God's grace because it recognizes itself to be a gathering of 'beggars' [Luther] which clings to the cross of Christ for its salvation. Therefore its service to

God is not efficacious because of its freedom from sin, but in spite of its unworthiness." *Theological Reflections on Ministry & Sexual Orientation* (Burlington: Trinity Press, 1990). For a critique of this book, see the author's review in *Christian Week*, 11 June 1991.

10. John Stott, *Issues Facing Christians Today* (London: Marshalls, 1984), 316.

11. A ceasefire was signed between warring factions nine months after this visit. However, following a national election in 1992, fighting resumed.

12. Of the more than thirty-five images of the church found in the New Testament, "new creation" is one. See 2 Cor. 5:17.

13. "The primary task given to the company of His followers by the risen Lord, before His ascension into heaven, was the task of making the gospel known to the ends of the earth. World-wide evangelism, therefore, was from the first, and still is, the chief task of the Church militant here on earth, in order that the elect community, which Christ died to redeem, may continually be added to, and ultimately made complete." Alan Stibbs, *God's Church* (London: IVF, 1959), 70.

Increasingly, Christian leaders are admitting that while evangelization must be primary, the gospel includes ministry to the whole person. In *Mission Trends*, No. 2 (New York: Paulist Press & Grand Rapids: William B. Eerdmans, 1975), John Stott writes: "The reason for social responsibility is not in order to give the gospel a credibility it would otherwise lack but simple uncomplicated compassion. Love does not need to justify itself . . .

Humanization, development, wholeness, liberation, justice: let me say at once that all these are not only desirable goals, but that Christians should be actively involved in pursuing them, and that we evangelicals have often been guilty of opting out of such social and political responsibilities" (8, 17). In the same book Philip A. Potter, then General Secretary of the World Council of Churches, wrote: "There has ... been a general agreement on what evangelization is not. First, it is not propaganda or the purveying of a particular confessional doctrine or way of life or of a so-called superior Christian culture to the exclusion of others ... the heart of the matter is [that] there must be personal encounter with Christ ... For on this relationship to God in Christ depends the eternal destiny of man" (166).

14. William Barclay, *The Plain Man Looks at the Apostles' Creed* (London: Collins/Fontana, 1967), 270.

15. Although "servant church" is a phrase often heard today, Avery Dulles comments: "While service is often extolled, the Bible does not seem to envision the task of the Church as service ... Neither Christ nor the Christian is supposed to be the world's servant. Jesus is obedient, not to the world but to the Father. He is the servant of God, not of men, and we too are called to be servants of God. ... The term *diakonia* is certainly one of the most important New Testament terms applied to the Church. The term applies to all types of ministry—including the ministry of the word, of sacraments, and of temporal help. All offices in the Church are forms of *diakonia,* and thus the term, in biblical usage, cannot properly be used in opposition to preaching or worship." Dulles does, however, see in the Servant Songs of Isaiah, and their use

in the New Testament, an "indirect foundation" for the concept of the servant church. *Models of the Church* (Garden City: Image Books/Doubleday, 1978), 104–106.

16. The Smalcald Articles, Part 3, XII.

17. "The end of the persecutions did not mean that the world had accepted the ideals of Christ and altered its ways; the world continued to prefer the darkness to the light (John 3:19). But if the world was no longer the enemy of the Christian, then the Christian had to become the enemy of the dark world. The flight to the desert was the way to escape a tempting conformity to the world. Here [the Desert Fathers] became a new kind of martyr: witnesses against the destructive powers of evil, witnesses for the saving power of Christ." Henri J. M. Nouwen, *The Way of the Heart* (New York: Ballantine Books, 1981), 3.

10. Finger in the Sand

1. Sherwood Eliot Wirt, *Love Song, A Fresh Translation of St. Augustine's Confessions* (New York: Harper & Row, 1971), 27–31.

2. M. Scott Peck, *People of the Lie* (New York: Simon and Schuster, 1983), 83.

3. J.N.D. Kelly, *Early Christian Doctrines* (London: Adam & Charles Black, 1958), 217–219.

4. Jan Milic Lochman, *The Faith We Confess, An Ecumenical Dogmatics,* trans. David Lewis (Philadelphia: Fortress, 1984), 223.

5. Charles Colson, *Loving God* (Grand Rapids: Zondervan, 1983), 27–34.

6. Ken Wilber, *No Boundary: Eastern and Western Approaches to Personal Growth* (Boulder: Shambhala, 1981), 24, 157.

7. Jean-Louis Louba, ed., *The Faith of the Church. A Commentary on the Apostles' Creed according to Calvin's Catechism,* trans. G. Vahanian (London: Collins/Fontana Books, 1960), 133, quoted in Lochman, *The Faith We Confess,* 224.

8. "Two things seem certain: (1) This is a true story about Jesus; and (2) it is not a true part of John's Gospel. The case against its traditional place in John at 7:53 is threefold: (a) The passage does not occur at all in many of our oldest and best manuscripts. (b) Its style and vocabulary resemble that of the earlier Gospels, especially Luke. (c) In its traditional place it breaks the sequence of the narrative. Evidently the story about Jesus and the adulteress was handed down orally in the Church; but because its teaching seemed to encourage lax treatment of sinners, it failed to win a place in the canonical scriptures. Later, when church discipline grew less severe, it returned to favour—and a place in the Gospels. For this we may well be grateful: few stories are more authentically stamped with 'Christ's touch.'" A. M. Hunter, *The Gospel According to John,* The Cambridge Bible Commentary (Cambridge: The Cambridge University Press, 1965), 199–200.

9. For the Mosaic Law on accused adulteresses, see Lev. 20:10 and Deut. 22:21ff.

10. For a summary of interpretations on the entire story, see J. C. Ryle, *Expository Thoughts on the Gospels, John,* vol. II (London: James Clarke, 1957), 73–83.

11. I am indebted to my editor, Denyse O'Leary, for this illuminating suggestion.

12. William Barclay, *The Gospel of John,* rev. ed., vol. 2 (Philadelphia: The Westminster Press, 1975), 7.

13. "When Jesus lived on earth, people found it very hard to believe that he really loved sinners. The inveterate belief even of most Christians is that God really loves respectable people; they find it very hard to believe that he stands on the side of sinners, rags and all . . . [But Jesus] stands in with [us]—not as a policeman to guard against future transgressions, not as an intolerably superior person contrasting his own virtue with the soiled reputation of the other, but as the friend who lives in hope, and rejoices in every sign that the healing power of his love and friendship is having the intended effect." Stephen Neill, *The Supremacy of Jesus* (Downers Grove: InterVarsity Press, 1984), 150–151.

14. Helmut Thielicke, *Our Heavenly Father* (New York: Harper & Brothers, 1960), 110.

15. "Neither is the effect of Christ's ordinance taken away by the wickedness [of evil ministers], nor the grace of God's gifts diminished from such as by faith and rightly do receive the sacraments ministered to them; which be effectual, because of Christ's institution and promise, although they be ministered by evil men." Arti-

cle XXVI, The (Thirty-Nine) Articles of Religion, *Book of Common Prayer.*

16. Peter Kreeft, *The Fundamentals of the Faith* (San Francisco: Ignatius, 1988), 222.

17. Helen Gardner, ed., *The Faber Book of Religious Verse* (London: Faber, 1972), 132.

11. Unfinished Symphony

1. "The sense of aging and mortality is accentuated by the change in generational status." Daniel J. Levinson, *The Seasons of a Man's Life* (New York: Ballantine Books, 1978), 214.

2. Incidence of suicide tripled between the 1950s and the 1980s, reported a TV special in October 1983. Suicide is the second leading cause of death among college students. One in eighty attempt it and one in eight thousand succeed!

3. Levinson, *Seasons of a Man's Life,* 216.

4. Dr. Robert Haynes, as quoted in John Naisbitt and Patricia Aburdene, *Megatrends 2000* (New York: Avon Books, 1990), 279.

5. Naisbitt and Aburdene, *Megatrends,* 288.

6. J. B. Priestley, *Time and the Conways* (London: Penguin, 1939), 60–61. Used by permission of Peters, Fraser, & Dunlop, London.

7. Lewis said that he would have given up on his pursuit of a personal, objective, living God and gladly accepted pantheism's subjective "God of beauty, truth and goodness, inside our own heads . . . a formless life-force surging through us, a vast power which we can tap" except that "There comes a moment when the children who have been playing at burglars hush suddenly: was that a *real* footstep in the hall? There comes a moment when people who have been dabbling in religion ('Man's search for God!') suddenly draw back. Supposing we really found Him? We never meant it to come to *that!* Worse still, supposing He had found us?" *Miracles* (London: Geoffrey Bles, 1957), 113–114.

8. J. W. C. Wand, *A History of the Early Church to A.D. 500* (London: Methuen, 1957), 136–138.

9. "The heroes of the mysteries were mythical figures, [but] the hero of the Christian 'myth' (if that word be permitted in this context) was an actual historical figure, of quite recent history, whose words and actions could be attested by surviving eye-witnesses." John Marsh, *Saint John,* Pelican Gospel Commentary series (Baltimore: Penguin, 1968), 37.

10. See Timothy L. Smith, *Revivalism & Social Reform* (New York: Harper & Row, 1965). "Contrary to the view that the holiness movement represented a flight from temporal realities, most of its leaders held optimistic views of a temporal millennium and of the necessity of social action to achieve it," 232.

11. Peter Kreeft, *Fundamentals of the Faith* (San Francisco: Ignatius, 1988), 161.

12. From 1543 on, the English forms of the Creed reverted to the Eastern Church's rendering: "resurrection of the body."

13. See Edmund D. Cohen, *The Mind of the Bible Believer* (Buffalo: Prometheus Books, 1988), 289n.

14. Copyright 1975 by Lucia R. Walker, c/o St. Stephen's Episcopal Church, Sewickley, Pa. Used by permission.

15. Elisabeth Kübler-Ross, *Questions and Answers on Death and Dying* (New York: Macmillan, 1974), 35.

16. One of my readers objected at this point: "But God created death!" It would seem so, from creation *as we know it* with its seasonal cycles of birth and death. Scripture also says that God uses death for His larger purposes: God "kills and makes alive; He brings down to the grave and brings up" (1 Sam. 2:6). But the Bible nowhere says that God creates death. His creative and redemptive powers are completely life-giving.

17. C. F. Gellert, 1757, trans. Francis E. Cox, 1841, *Anglican Hymn Book* (London: Vine, 1965), 187.

18. Quoted in Jan Milic Lochman, *The Faith We Confess, An Ecumenical Dogmatics,* trans. David Lewis (Philadelphia: Fortress, 1984), 254.

19. *The Book of Common Prayer,* According to the use of the Anglican Church of Canada (Toronto: Anglican Book Centre, 1959), 58.